# DESIGNING YOUR DREAM HUSBAND

Amie Dockery has given us a well-written book presenting wonderful stories of Bible personalities—husbands with obvious flaws, but men whom God used in mighty ways. It is God who helps us to love and accept our husbands and see them as the men that God can help them become.

*Evelyn Roberts*

WIFE OF ORAL ROBERTS, FOUNDER AND CHANCELLOR OF ORAL ROBERTS UNIVERSITY

Amie Hayes Dockery has the knack; you know the one I'm talking about—that special gift for pulling it all together and creating something beautiful. That is exactly what this book is about. *Designing Your Dream Husband* creatively blends interior design tips with biblical character profiles laced with gift ideas to make truth pop off the page and into our hearts and marriages.

*Lisa Whelchel*

AUTHOR OF THE BEST-SELLER *CREATIVE CORRECTION*, AND *THE FACTS OF LIFE AND OTHER LESSONS MY FATHER TAUGHT ME*
FOUNDER, MOMTIME MINISTRIES

# DESIGNING YOUR Dream HUSBAND

# AMIE DOCKERY

**Regal**

From Gospel Light
Ventura, California, U.S.A.

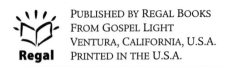

PUBLISHED BY REGAL BOOKS
FROM GOSPEL LIGHT
VENTURA, CALIFORNIA, U.S.A.
**Regal**   PRINTED IN THE U.S.A.

Regal Books is a ministry of Gospel Light, a Christian publisher dedicated to serving the local church. We believe God's vision for Gospel Light is to provide church leaders with biblical, user-friendly materials that will help them evangelize, disciple and minister to children, youth and families.

It is our prayer that this Regal book will help you discover biblical truth for your own life and help you meet the needs of others. May God richly bless you.

*For a free catalog of resources from Regal Books/Gospel Light, please call your Christian supplier or contact us at 1-800-4-GOSPEL or www.regalbooks.com.*

Cover design by David Griffing
Internal design by Stephen Hahn

**Library of Congress Cataloging-in-Publication Data**

Dockery, Amie.
  Designing your dream husband / Amie Dockery.
    p. cm.
  ISBN 0-8307-3633-6
  1. Men in the Bible—Biography. 2. Bible—Biography. 3. Mate selection—Religious aspects—Christianity. I. Title.
  BS571.5.D63 2004
  248.8'435—dc22                                                2004019219

1 2 3 4 5 6 7 8 9 10 11 12 13 14 15 / 10 09 08 07 06 05 04

Rights for publishing this book in other languages are contracted by Gospel Light Worldwide, the international nonprofit ministry of Gospel Light. Gospel Light Worldwide also provides publishing and technical assistance to international publishers dedicated to producing Sunday School and Vacation Bible School curricula and books in the languages of the world. For additional information, visit www.gospellightworldwide.org; write to Gospel Light Worldwide, P.O. Box 3875, Ventura, CA 93006; or send an e-mail to info@gospellightworldwide.org.

# DEDICATION

To my mother, for giving me aim,
and to my husband, for being a bull's-eye.

I love you both so much. With you two working together,
I may turn out all right after all!

# CONTENTS

# FOREWORD

Did you marry the perfect man on your wedding day only to discover there were quite a few things you would like to see changed after you had lived with him awhile?

Amie Hayes Dockery, in her book *Designing Your Dream Husband,* has given us a good view of the folly of such a notion. Many of the flaws we see in our husbands are prick points from the Lord that are meant to shape us up.

One story in my own life comes to mind. One of our friends married a lady that we knew well but with whom we had never had such close contact as when we were pastoring a small church in the Midwest. There was just something about this person that grated on me. One day, as I was praying about the situation and saying, *Lord, you need to change Peggy.\* Why don't you make her a more congenial individual? She would be so much easier to be with if she was not so arrogant and snooty and was a bit more down to earth,* a whisper came to my heart—and I knew it was the Lord. He said, "Maybe it's not her I want to change." From that time on, I had to check my attitude regarding Peggy and look inside myself to see what I needed to change so that our relationship could be as it should be.

Here is one of the principles in Amie's book that caught my attention: "The power in prayer doesn't come from praying your problems; it only comes in praying the answers." This statement makes me pray what I want to see happen with my husband, not the things I wish he would change.

Some time ago, I wrote down all of the positive qualities I could think of about my husband, Jack. Periodically, I still look

*not her real name

at that list and feel very fortunate and blessed that I have a husband who tells me often that he loves me, who is not a moody person at all, who is a good father to our children, and more. I would suggest that every wife do the same thing. It is good for the soul and also good for your marriage relationship.

Amie will give you suggestions, including suggested gifts that you may buy, to solidify your growth in the area you have just read about in each chapter. Her suggestions are so helpful in making the principles she teaches yours.

*Designing Your Dream Husband* is a good textbook to follow in every aspect of your marriage relationship. Amie writes about the things we really don't like to face, such as submission, communication, dedication and other weighty subjects that need to be practiced to cultivate a successful marriage. If you practice her suggestions, you will be amply rewarded for your effort. A happy marriage is certainly worth every effort we make.

Jack and I will celebrate our fiftieth wedding anniversary this year. Although we have had our disagreements, we have worked together to bring about a very happy union. It probably would have happened more easily if we had had a textbook like this to follow.

Anna Hayford

# ACKNOWLEDGMENTS

From the bottom of my heart, I wish to thank my mother, who was at least a full-time consultant on this book, and on some days looked more like a ghostwriter. Thank you so much for the all-nighters. I'm sorry they didn't end in my adolescence.

I would love to thank two wonderful women, Jackie Shepherd and Johanna Neesom, for their contribution to this project. Your dedication goes so far beyond human expectation and ability to calculate. I pray that God will grant you both the single thing you most desire.

To Judy Pogue, thank you for your candor and transparency. I want you to know that any time you talk, women young and old listen. And I must say thank you to Paul, your generous husband! If he weren't the walking, talking, modern version of Joseph, I wouldn't have believed so easily or prayed so fervently! I love you both and am so grateful that God brought you into my and my husband's lives.

Thank you to all the women in my life—Grandmother, aunts, cousins, friends and pastors' wives. Without your impartation, I would be completely unqualified and underdeveloped. You all make me credible. I love you!

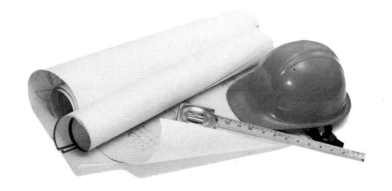

# CHAPTER I

# THE ART OF DESIGN

*Use wisdom and understanding to establish your home; let good sense fill
the rooms with priceless treasures.*
PROVERBS 24:3

God has given women a unique gift of vision. This gift is so
woven into a woman's nature that she often views life—from
home to husband—with the thought, *Wow, I could do great things
with that!* To see potential is a wonderful gift; but many times we,
as women, do not know how to get from where we are to where
we want to be. We want to see change, and we want to see it now!
I keenly understand the discouragement of comparing reality
with expectation.

During the early years of my marriage, I went about showing
my husband, Stacey, his potential—in all the wrong ways. I made
all the common mistakes, such as comparing him with other
great men of God and making sly suggestions. Although my

wholehearted intention was to build up my husband, I was actually tearing him down.

One day, I met a woman with a very successful husband whose personality was quite similar to my husband's. As she and I discussed her past, I asked her to describe how she had encouraged her husband to greatness. She simply said, "Years ago the Lord told me that I must be careful how I treat my husband, because he is a Joseph." I knew that her husband's name wasn't Joseph, so I asked her to explain what she meant. She told me that God had given her a picture of her husband's calling and anointing as similar to the character that Joseph displayed, recorded in the book of Genesis. Seeing her husband the way God saw him literally gave her a pattern to pray for him and gave her an expectancy about the fulfillment of his calling.

After that conversation, I realized that the real work in my marriage was going to take place in me. For the first time, I understood the influence that my view of my husband had upon my actions, primarily because I knew that I had not asked God to give me the picture of how *He* views my husband. Just the thought of being married to a Joseph, a Moses or a Daniel in the making held me to a new standard of support for my husband.

I was accustomed to picturing a desired outcome for my children's future before making any decision on how to raise them. So I don't know why I had never considered my actions as a path to the future partner I was "creating." The day I heard my friend speak of her husband as a Joseph, I came face-to-face with the reality of the destiny I was influencing for my husband through my expectations, or lack thereof. I began to think, *Wouldn't it be great for my husband to have the faith of Abraham, the integrity of Joseph, the heart of David, the leadership of Nehemiah and the purpose of Paul!*

As I began to seek God about the needed changes in my life, He gave me the techniques outlined in this book to teach me how to love and respect my husband by commissioning through prayer the Holy Spirit to do the work. I believe this book offers a biblical approach for a wife who wants to keep herself from destructive patterns of communication with her husband and to restore love, honor and respect to the way she interacts with him.

## Perspective and Destiny

Although the message of this book is wrapped in a design theme that will give you tips for transforming your home, inside are deep and penetrating truths from the Word of God that truly have the power to transform your life and your marriage if you will apply them. Although many of my comments are addressed to married women, the principles gleaned from Scripture are just as applicable to single women who are praying for God's guidance in the provision of a mate. Not only will this book help you, single woman, identify what to look for in a man, but its principles, when applied, also have the potential to show you what to do with him when you get him!

I certainly hope this book will be a resource to those of you who are mothers as well. It's never too early to start teaching your young daughters how to become women who will create a loving home and a strong marriage through reliance on the grace and power of the Lord.

When I was a young girl of about 14, my mother challenged me to make a list of specific qualities I would want in a husband. I immediately put my diary to good use. When I read the list to my mother, she told me to keep the list open for adding qualities that would become important to me as I grew older. She also stressed the importance of praying about these requests and about the man who would come to possess these attributes. The practice of keeping this list reinforced my hope and faith that God was patterning the perfect partner for me. Sometime later, I began writing letters to my future husband. These letters primarily contained little daily experiences I wished to share with the man who would truly treasure them one day.

Years later, when my husband and I were moving into a new house, I found my letters, journals and diaries in an old box. When I realized what I had found, I was elated to share these letters with the man to whom I had written them. The most precious of these love notes was one titled "I Choose You." In this letter, I had explained that the most popular boy in my biology class had invited me to homecoming. I had been torn about what to do. Should I go with him? After all, it was only a date. Would this decision change my destiny? Finally, at the end of the letter, I had scribbled, "I choose you—my future."

Letting my husband read this letter was a precious experience that gave him a peek into my developing heart and soul as a 16-year-old girl who already belonged to him long before he met me.

I don't think I would have written these letters so faithfully and thus felt the release to make the best decisions about dating had my mother not been there to support me. She could have made me think I was just a silly girl with dreamy eyes and laughed at me for focusing so much attention on the future, but she didn't. She gave me a plan for investing in my future marriage, which I now know kept me from many destructive decisions that could have changed my destiny.

# How to Use This Book

Every principle in this book is ignited through prayer and practical application. So if you are single, applying these principles can be as effective in creating the marriage you desire as if you were applying them to the actual experience. You don't need to know your husband's name to pray for him and to pray for his destiny and calling. Know this: Prayer knows no distance, and God honors the investment of time. What an awesome marriage foundation you will have by preparing yourself right now and praying that God will do the same for your future mate! I will give some special instruction for how singles can apply their prayer investment in the "Seal It with a Gift" sections in later chapters.

Let me explain the contents and flow of each part division and chapter within each part division. There are seven part divisions in this book named for an element of design: Perspective, Unity, Creativity, Authenticity, Balance, Function and Illumination. All of these elements, vital to a home's interior design, are equally relevant to the design of human relationships. Part 1 begins with the design element of perspective and discusses who will be your design Dream Team and what are the best tools for design, as well as provides insight into God's master plan for marriage.

In parts 2 through 6, you will find that each chapter outlines a character study from the Bible and the mantle (the gift of impartation of both identity and authority) that God bestowed on each of these men. I have divided these chapters into three major sections: Making the Mantle, Missing the Mantle and Modeling the Mantle. In Making the Mantle, we will see how experiences formed the character of the man. In Missing the Mantle, we will explore how the man was made vulnerable either through the absence of the mantle or through the personality of the mantle itself. In Modeling the Mantle, we will see the ideal expression of the anointing that the mantle provides.

As you read about these biblical men, you will be able to match your husband's character and mantle with one or more of these profiles. By recognizing the similarities between your husband and these honored men of faith, you can gain insight into the vulnerabilities that could cause your husband to miss the blessing of the mantle, as well as insight into what will help him fully realize the anointing upon his life. Although your husband will naturally carry more attributes of one particular mantle, I challenge you to give each of the mantles equal time. Your prayer of impartation will bring balance and covering for your husband in many areas as well as bring him closer in likeness to the perfect man—Jesus—who demonstrated the power of wearing each mantle with authority.

To test your knowledge and encourage you to go deeper, I have included in each chapter a section called "Questions to Consider." You may answer these questions aloud, but I recommend that you record your answers in a journal and use them during prayer.

Next in the flow of each chapter is the "Authority at a Glance" section. This bulleted list recaps each mantle's qualities and describes how these qualities affect the person who wears that particular mantle.

After all the materials of knowledge are gathered, it is time to start the building process through prayer. To help you begin this process, I have included a section called "Pattern for Prayer." Although the form may be a bit different each time you pray, patterns are simple to follow and can be used as a future prayer reference. After you pray, you will make a declaration—a statement of your vision for yourself and your husband—as you choose to take on a new view of the future. Step by step, as one action leads to another, the actions become increasingly practical. Taking action is a pattern of behavior in itself; it is absolutely crucial that we bring our flesh in line with our spirit.

The last step in these chapters of biblical profiles is the "Seal It with a Gift" section. I have found that a person cannot give impartation in a more practical and beautiful way than by giving a gift. I hope you will fully enjoy completing this step. (Most women welcome another reason to shop!) For married women, there is also a list of suggestions for buying tokens for husbands associated with each mantle.

For single women, the shopping begins now! I would like to suggest that a very special way of treasuring your prayer investment is by assembling a unique hope chest, or treasure chest. Your first purchase will be the treasure chest—a decorative box such as a small hatbox, a closable coffee table/nightstand box or a beautiful Bible box. Whatever you choose, make sure that your treasure chest pleases you visually. The chest needs to speak to you whenever you see it, so be sure that you know exactly where you are going to place it in your home. You could set it on top of your nightstand, near your bathtub, on your coffee table or beside your prayer chair. I would also encourage you to purchase the chest with ceremony and make the day special by combining its purchase with some of your favorite experiences: lunch with a friend, a manicure and pedicure, a visit to a favorite coffee bar—let your imagination soar. Have fun with this! It will become one of the most prayerfully constructed gifts you ever have the pleasure of giving to your future mate. (What an engagement gift this would make!)

I am continually amazed at the detail to which our prayers are answered if we take the time to be specific. My prayer for you is that this book will give you more focus in the art of praying effectively for your husband. And for those of you who are single, you have even more time to perfect the art of design and the process of building (prayer) for your future mate. Are you ready to begin? Then let's get started!

*Design Element:*

# PERSPECTIVE

*God blesses those people whose hearts are pure. They will see him!*

MATTHEW 5:8

*Fine art is that in which the hand, the head
and the heart of man go together.*

JOHN RUSKIN

I have paintings, prints and pictures throughout my house, each of which captures a special moment or feeling and represents a concept that goes beyond the beauty or the color of the image displayed. One such print, which I purchased at the Palace of Versailles in Paris, portrays the beauty of Josephine, Napoleon's wife, elegantly bowing her head as she is crowned the empress of Rome. The story behind the painting captures the overarching concept of this book.

When Napoleon desired to be the emperor of Rome, he knew that he could not crown himself. Although he took possession of foreign soil without blinking an eye, he must have realized that the title of emperor could not be forcibly obtained. Such an act would have seemed greedy, and this would have been unacceptable to his loyal subjects. Besides, the title of emperor was an honor that should be bestowed by the people. Napoleon must have recognized that the instrument of power he did wield was the authority to crown others of noble esteem. He, therefore, crowned his wife, Josephine, the empress of Rome. As a result, he became the emperor of Rome. It was through his marriage that this authority was made possible. By the simple act of empowering his partner, he was raised to the next level as well. Napoleon's intentions may have been for his own gain, but the principle is still the same. If you honor those around you, your life will be elevated as well.

Perhaps the greatest obstacle to this principle within marriage is a widely held belief that we must respect everything about our husbands in order to honor them.

This is not true. We do not have to respect performance to honor position. The actions of respecting and honoring are fundamentally different because respect and honor are not reactions, they are demonstrations of perspective.

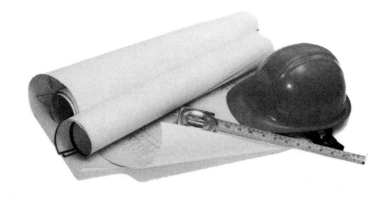

# CHAPTER 2

# AN EYE FOR DESIGN

*I never saw an ugly thing in my life: for let the form of an object be what it may—light, shade, and perspective will always make it beautiful.*

JOHN CONSTABLE

I love using the elements of design as symbols for the concepts taught in this book, primarily because there are spiritual principles at work in the methods of design. And what better way to learn these principles than by combining the two things that make us feel so very feminine—our men and our ideas?

If you are a woman who lives for the thrill of putting projects together and seeing your vision come to life, then the concepts of design will not be foreign to you. Just being alive affords us opportunities to design many delightful things, not the least of which are our destinies.

When it comes to design, you may or may not see yourself as having an eye for it. So before you become cautious with the term "design," let me explain how perfectly you were made for the job of designer.

## Little Girl's Dream

The art of design is captured by seeing the big picture and then bringing the elements of vision and action together. In other words, design begins with vision and ends with practical application. Some of us are avid dreamers, while others of us focus on the daily details of life. Both of these attributes are pivotal to success in design, but each attribute has its own purpose. As we begin this book, I want you to focus on dreaming. To dream is to birth ideas that grow into vision.

Little girls are born to dream. From the earliest moments of my childhood, I dreamed of being married and having babies. I have never met a little girl who didn't dream about what she would like to be when she grew up.

If your strength is in accomplishing daily tasks, then you may have abandoned long ago your days of dreaming. If you are still a dreamer, then you may have put your heart on hold because of discouragement. Either way, I want you to get in touch with the dreamer inside of you.

Try to remember some of the dreams you had in childhood. Do you remember how those dreams made you feel? Now that you're a grown woman, have you stopped dreaming—stopped believing—that anything is possible?

I have a group of friends who take big risks when they decorate their homes. This courage seems to be rare among most women, but I think this particular group of friends find it primarily through the camaraderie they have found in each other's company. When one of the women announces her desire to do something drastic, everyone else encourages the idea once it has been thoroughly and passionately portrayed.

I want to offer you the same kind of support as you read this book. Although I will not encourage you to paint your house in a rainbow of colors, I will push you to dream without limits. I want you to live fully within the creative mind that God has given you. Just think, I can plant a thought, and you can create a wonderfully detailed scene in your mind that would take millions of dollars to re-create in a movie theater. We are going to use that same power of vision to frame your future by picturing in the present.

I am by nature a visionary, which can be a great source of frustration for me if my comparison between what is and what can be doesn't lead me to a plan. I may see the design in my mind by dreaming of the future; but unless I have a way of bringing the future into the present, I get bogged down.

When I experience this frustration, I force myself to examine exactly when and where my dreams were derailed. Often I have found that I'm most vulnerable to this confusion when I fail to record my ideas. By listing my likes and dislikes about the current situation, I free my mind to move a step ahead of where I am. It is very simple, but great plans always are. Remember that no matter how detailed the plan may be, you will get there by putting one foot in front of the other. Let's begin right now to take that first simple step into the future.

## The Power of a Picture

The specific ability to hear, understand and apply words to a mental picture is the groundwork for design in any arena. In the world of design, the term "perspective" is used to gain visual background from which to build the future. In a spiritual sense, perspective combines vision and position. That is why perspective is the first design element we will consider. How we view what we see in our minds has a fundamental effect on subsequent layers of thought. When we bring physical design in line with the spirit, we define "perspective" as "picturing."

I will ask you to practice picturing by doing some creative but simple tasks.

## Framing the Future

This exercise will leave you with a picture of those things you may not have the courage to say out loud. Now, I realize that doing crafts may not be your thing. But trust me; I don't spend time creating things that will not inspire me again and again. I keep my framed future on my bedside table, along with my favorite books. Every time I look at the pictures I have chosen to represent my dreams, I say to myself, *That's me!* I have seen the manifestation of some of the dreams I dared to picture, and I cannot encourage you strongly enough to gather your craft items, get comfortable with a cup of coffee or tea and begin this exercise.

### Items Needed:

- scissors, glue, old magazines
- One piece of 8x10 card stock
- Presentation binder with clear overlay on front and see-through inner pockets
- Medium-wide ribbon or colored paper (optional)

**Instructions:** Peruse magazines for pictures of elements that describe your dreams for the future and cut them out. Take your time. You are looking for symbols that represent your desires. You will be surprised by how many things remind you of your dreams and aspirations. When you have found enough images, make a collage of your pictures by gluing them on the card stock. Let the images flow together with edges overlapping. You can finish this exercise by making a frame from ribbon or colored paper. When you are finished, slide the picture into the front see-through overlay of your binder. This is your dream book for the future. All exercises in later chapters will find their home within the pages of your binder.

I am providing this exercise because I believe in the power of seeing your dreams. Describing your dreams in words is partially effective, but it doesn't have the same impact as visual stimuli. I have received many testimonies of women who participated in this exercise several years ago at one of our church's ladies' retreats. Each woman's story is different, but the theme is the same: Once each woman saw her dreams in color, she could no longer deny her destiny. This exercise had forced these women to face their obstacles and to form a plan to realize their dreams.

## The Power of Perspective

Sometimes the quickest route to a positive perspective and the formation of a plan to realize your dreams is to take an objective seat. See your marriage as a whole, viewing the partnership in both the present and the future.

Let's take inventory. First, identify which room in your home is the one you like the least. Grab a chair, two pieces of paper and a pen, and go to that room. Choose a position in the room where you can see everything clearly. Take a look around the room and describe on paper your design dilemma (make a list of your dislikes regarding the room). Absolutely everything in the room can make the list, but don't just write, "Hate furniture"; describe what it is about the furniture that is unsightly. For example, you could write: "The furniture is too dark and too small, and it has no shape." When you are finished, fold the piece of paper and place it under your chair.

Take the second piece of paper and sit for a moment to dream of all this room could be if everything but its structure could be changed. Describe the dream in detail. It is important to use descriptive sentences to put your vision into words. Don't leave out anything regarding your desire for this room's outcome. The following questions may help you: How would you change the layout of the furniture? What color would you paint the walls? What functions could this room provide for your family if money were no object?

## Focus Out Frustration

Now you have two pieces of paper with very different descriptions. One piece of paper contains the reality of the present; the other contains the reality of the future. One piece of paper lists the negative aspects of the room and the other defines your desires. Which of the two pieces of paper is more useful to help you move toward your goal? Would you revisit the list of dislikes many times to remind yourself of what needs to be changed? No, you already know what you don't like about this room. You probably think about your dislikes every time you use the room. The purpose of the first list is to get your concerns on paper and out of your mind.

Thinking that the negative list gives you power to change the future is as futile as reminding your husband of everything he does wrong while expecting him to change. How many times do you need to discuss your dislikes? If you are single, focusing on the present situation will only serve to discourage and disappoint you. You must face your current reality, but you cannot stay there! Getting the picture for your future requires that you abandon your opinions of the present and put your energy into the future.

In the past, I was frightened to allow myself to admit what was bothering me about my marriage. I was afraid that if I vocalized my concerns, I would suffer more from admitting my current dissatisfaction. So I wrote my concerns in a prayer journal. To my surprise, I felt an immediate release and consequently experienced a level of illumination previously unavailable to me. By writing my dislikes about the present and my hopes for the future, I set myself up for accountability through prayer. Very quickly, my venting on paper grew in to pouring my heart out before the Lord.

You are probably thinking that my husband's faults were my main focus; not so! In fact, I felt freedom to talk about my own deficiencies in great detail and without judgment. There is a definite release when you list your concerns on paper. But power in prayer doesn't come from praying for your problems; it comes from praying for the answers. I always come away from one of these prayer letters with a renewed sense of perspective about my life and a new appreciation for my husband. If you are unmarried, I would encourage you to focus your prayers on the desires of your heart (see Ps. 37:4) and the growth you hope to see in yourself in the future.

## Prayer: Putting Your Words to Work

Regular and thorough prayer should be part of your daily routine. After a worship time in the morning, I pray verbally throughout the day. I like to turn on worship music as I prepare for the day, letting it play until I leave the house. Sometimes worship comes over me, and I must stop what I am doing to fully experience the Spirit in my home. Other times, I dance throughout the house as I pick up laundry and do some cleaning. I like to think of this as spiritual housecleaning. In order to make different methods of prayer part of your daily routine, I encourage you to incorporate these times into your other activities. Why waste time just folding clothes when you can cover your family with prayer while you fold?

Although I worship and pray throughout the day, I traditionally write my prayers at night, which suits my schedule and personality. During a bath or bedtime ritual, I allow the Lord to cleanse my mind as I put words to paper. Your best time for writing may be in the morning while drinking a cup of coffee or during your children's nap time in the afternoon. Whatever the time of day, take at least 10 minutes of peace and quiet while you write.

Right now, I would like you to pray on paper by listing your concerns on one sheet and your dreams for the future on another. Concentrate on your marriage as a whole, not just on your role or your husband's role. Here are a few examples to help you along. "Dilemma: Lord, I am concerned by the lack of joy we experience as a couple. We used to laugh, and I miss that about our relationship. Dream: Lord, I see You using us together to encourage other couples that have been discouraged by financial pressure."

## A Mirror Image

As we have already seen, first we address perspective when we dream; then we consider position. Understanding that any vision comes from a specific position automatically relegates it to certain restraints. Consider the function and placement of a mirror. The mirror cannot reflect a room from many different perspectives; it is limited to reflecting what is directly in front of it. However, a mirror is used to open up a room by expanding the room's reflective surfaces. But a mirror has limitations; its impact is only as powerful as what it reflects. If you hang a mirror at a high position, then you will want to tilt it downward so that it doesn't reflect a blank ceiling but instead gives you a loftier view of a room. If you place a mirror on a mantel, you must also put decorative items in front of it so that the mirror is a useful focal point that adds dimension to the room.

Husbands and wives serve as mirrors for one another. We cannot see ourselves clearly; thus, we need covenant relationships that can be both transparent and reflective. Very often the things we pick on in our partners are attributes we dislike in ourselves. If you were a mirror for your husband, would it not be your responsibility to clean the debris from your life so that he could see himself more clearly?

This thinking may seem backward to you. But just like a mirror's reflection, everything we see in life is the reflection of our perspective. To change your perspective, you must change your position. I want you to realize how limited you will be if you don't begin to see yourself the way God sees you—from a higher vantage point.

## Design Demonstration Exercise

Find a mirror; it doesn't need to be large. I would suggest that you try this exercise with a mirror you already have. If you like the result, you can buy a mirror to fill the space permanently. A tall armoire or bookcase that doesn't touch the ceiling would be the best location for our experiment. Place the mirror on top of the piece of furniture at an angle to the corner. Do not center the mirror; instead place it to one side. Achieve a forward tilt of the mirror by placing a stack of books in front of it on one side. The height of the stack of books can control the level of angle. Once the mirror is in an agreeable position, add a tall candlestick, glass vase or piece of pottery and an arrangement of greenery. Place one of the items on top of the stack of books. (Always use accessories in odd-numbered amounts; three items are best for this design.) Play with variations on this design for a while; it takes time to be at ease with the role of designer.

If you succeed at pleasing your eye with this test, then you may choose to keep this dramatic focal point for your room. If you are unsure about the effect, ask a girlfriend for her opinion. Don't give up after the first try. Experiment with different looks by placing other knickknacks in front of the mirror to change the design.

You may feel uncomfortable with change, not only when it comes to design, but also in your marriage. Seeing yourself as the catalyst, or change agent, is not an easy adjustment. So we will take it in stages. If you leave the mirror in its lofty position, you will find yourself looking up more often than you did before. Either way, this design tip demonstrates how different the angle of your perspective can be, based on your position. And every time you see your work, I hope that you will recall how important it is to take on God's eye for design.

## Get the Picture?

**For Married Women:** Your position within your marriage has always been vital; but how you view your position, especially in the role of change agent, is where the power lies. Simply knowing who you are and what role you play makes all the difference between a disaster and a well-carried-out design.

**For Unmarried Women:** Ask God to give you His perspective of the single season you are in. Although you are not yet joined to your husband in the natural realm, your destinies are intertwined in the spiritual realm. Therefore, every decision or choice will impact the marriage that is your future calling.

There is a reason that God has not yet brought you and your future husband together. It is vital that you remain faithful to this time of preparation by petitioning God to make you aware of anything you need to work on. These words are not meant to insinuate that you are flawed but simply to say that God is working in both your life and your future husband's life to achieve the proper balance and dynamic for your future marriage. Applying daily prayer preparation now will yield a supernatural connection with your husband from the beginning of your marriage.

# CHAPTER 3

# WHAT EVERY DESIGNER NEEDS

*Proper words in proper places make the true definition of style.*
JONATHAN SWIFT

Even if you are uncertain about your ability as a designer, when it comes to designing your dream husband, you are the expert. You don't feel like an expert? Don't worry—you won't be working alone. Let me introduce you to your design team.

## Call In the Experts

Your design team is made up of four experts: architect, supplier, builder and designer.

**The Architect:** Jeremiah 29:11 declares, "I will bless you with a future filled with hope—a future of success, not of suffering." And Jeremiah 1:5 (*NIV*) declares, "Before I formed you in the womb I knew you, before you were born I set you apart."

Almighty God, the creator of the universe, designed a perfect plan for each of us. Only He knows every detail of our lives, and how and when those details will come together to produce our destiny. This means that God had a blueprint before He created you. You were created for a purpose, according to a master plan. The practical way to receive this plan from God is to read His Word, the most wondrous life instruction book ever written. The Bible leads us toward monumental growth and also gives us direction for the smaller details in life. Not only has our Architect originated a wonderful blueprint for our lives, but He also has orchestrated the effort to bring it to pass.

**The Supplier:** "I pray that God will take care of all your needs with the wonderful blessings that come from Christ Jesus!" (Phil. 4:19).

Jesus Christ gave His life to provide us with all that we need in order to fulfill the will of God. He showed His commitment to quality by enduring the worst—taking on the past, present and future sin of the world when He died on the cross—so that we could have the best. Not only did Jesus sacrifice to pay the price for us, but He also serves now as the middleman for material negotiations. The Word of God tells us that He ever lives to make intercession for us (see Heb. 7:25). This means that He works day and night to prepare for the next level of labor in our lives.

**The Builder:** "And you are part of that building Christ has built as a place for God's own Spirit to live" (Eph. 2:22).

The Holy Spirit is sent to oversee the day-to-day operation

and productivity of our lives. Though He conducts activity undercover, His main objective is to carry out the plans of the Architect. The Holy Spirit is commissioned to do the specific work of building up the dream through encouragement and exhortation; He remains on-site at all times, providing team spirit: "God is wonderful and glorious. I pray that his Spirit will make you become strong followers" (Eph. 3:16).

**The Designer:** "Then the LORD told me: 'I will give you my message in the form of a vision. Write it clearly enough to be read at a glance'" (Hab. 2:2).

The position of designer—that's you—is pivotal to the implementation of the master plan set forth by the Architect. The designer's responsibility is to consult the design team regularly for direction concerning the divine plan. The designer's job is also to document the process, pray about the plan and apply the vision.

You may feel unworthy to work with such an accomplished and honorable team. Our levels of experience make it pretty obvious that we are not worthy on our own merit. God cares about us so much that He listens to our petitions and gives us authority to make life work because we are working to fulfill *His* plan.

We do not walk in the proper authority when we are rarely and randomly in position. Nor do we have power to produce our own design. We are appointed and commissioned to fulfill a certain course of action according to a plan. To do this, we must walk at a level of submission worthy of authority. The power of the kingdom of God is a secret to those who do not understand that authority in the Spirit comes only from the sacrifice of submission. To reach a higher level of authority, one must reach a greater level of submission. This is how the least shall be greatest in the kingdom of God, which ultimately means that God has put Himself in submission to us.

I'll admit that the statement I just made may sound shocking. But stay with me here. It is absolutely true that God carries all power and authority. At the same time, He has limited His authority by submitting His control to our free will. This means that He will not step in and take over our role. In this way, He has submitted to us Himself and all that He has to offer. Because all the members of the design team work in submission to one another, we are part of that equation. Accepting His will, submitting to His plan and receiving the reward are decisions and actions that we must apply to our role.

Can you grasp that thought? It just doesn't get any better than this! We have been paired with the original Dream Team, and they are waiting to meet with us right now.

## Team Meeting Agenda:
## The Designer's Commitment

Let's approach this Dream Team meeting in the form of a prayer, broken down phrase by phrase. The statements in the following section are meant to prompt you to deeper thought and response. Feel free to use the prayer points as a place to begin; but don't just read them. Your conversations with God will move forward as you make this prayer your own through writing your thoughts and using your own words and experiences. Before you begin reading the following bullet points aloud, have your journal handy to write down the specifics of your life. For example, in the first prayer point, we address the area of acknowledging God as our beginning. To add more detail to your prayer, you might write something like this:

Lord, I want You to know that I have never really considered Your desire to be involved in every area of my life.

I am just beginning to realize that You have concentrated Your efforts on every detail of my destiny. Please forgive me for trying to do Your job. I do trust You! I want You to have Your way in the fulfillment of the plan that You have designed for my life.

A fundamental reason to pray is to build relationship with God, so remember to keep your prayer conversational and to speak to Him as you would to your closest friend. Although God knows our every thought, we still must pray to confess our sin and to show our faith. It is vital that God knows, and that we know, where we stand. You can let Him know by voicing simple statements of faith.

You wouldn't tell your spouse only once that you love him, check it off your to-do list and move on, would you? I know it may sound silly to make this comparison, but how many of us have thought, *God knows I love Him, so why do I have to tell Him?* Just because God doesn't demand our daily commitment does not mean that He isn't desirous and appreciative of our affirmation of love and devotion. We need to live the fire and passion we feel for God every day and wholeheartedly communicate it to Him! You may enter God's throne room with only a moment's notice. What a great honor that He is anticipating your arrival! Are you ready?

In preparation for prayer, I suggest that you go where you feel most comfortable—an easy chair, a blanket on the floor or a cozy couch.

## Prayer of Commitment

⅋ Dear Father, I acknowledge You as the Architect of my life and the creator of my purpose.

- I thank You for your patience and diligence in pursuing me.
- Please forgive me for neglecting to consult You on the plans You have for my life.
- Your Word says that all I have to do is ask in order to receive direction (see Prov. 3:5-6).
- Today I ask that You show me the plans You have for me.
- I know that the house You build is great, because You are great above all gods (see 2 Chron. 2:5).
- Forgive me for ignoring Your instructions in the past.
- Forgive me for the times I have taken over.
- Bring balance to my perspective through the revelation of Your Word.
- I give You my dreams for the future and ask that You establish within them Your perfect will and timing.
- Renew my opportunities, ignite my desires, and energize my unfulfilled dreams.
- I want to live according to Your plan.
- I submit my time, my trust and my treasures to You.
- Let me bring glory every day to the honor of being a wife.
- Your Word says, "Use wisdom and understanding to establish your home; let good sense fill the rooms with priceless treasures" (Prov. 24:3-4).
- Lord, please give me wisdom to build, and keep me from destruction. I want Your will to be established in my life and my marriage.
- Holy Spirit, transform me. I will yield control and allow You to do Your work in my spirit. My greatest desire is that I come to a place of maturity in Christ Jesus. Amen.

# Choosing the Perfect Tools

It is so gratifying to have the proper tool for a specific task. I recently received a little gadget that slices through cellophane CD wrappers. What used to break a fingernail now takes a simple swish of the blade. These days there are tools for just about every need. Traditional tools are made for physical tasks, but there are spiritual tools fashioned for specific jobs as well. The worst thing we can do is to use the wrong tool and do more damage than good. Let's go through our spiritual toolbox to identify what we will use and what we will not use. Although I have tailored this analogy for married women, these principles will apply to every relationship. If you are single, I encourage you to evaluate your relationship toolbox now, while there's no one looking over your shoulder. Just think about how prepared you'll be; and your future husband may never know that he could have married a "drill" sergeant!

**Hammer:** This tool represents the act of forcing our will on our husbands. Even if the message is redeeming, the method is destructive. We won't need to hammer on our husbands, so put this tool away.

**Nails:** We don't need to use words that pierce and wound. Unguarded words should be viewed as highly dangerous sharp objects that we don't want to leave lying around.

**Screwdriver:** This tool is one to consider using. Some of us may need to loosen up! It's possible that we are so tightly wound that we overreact to situations and fly off the handle. Although circumstances can cause us to be tense, we must make the choice to relax about things that won't really matter in the long run.

**Measuring Tape:** This tool represents man's potential as a whole and how our husbands stand in comparison. As we put this tool away in our toolbox, we also put away the ability to measure

our husbands against others and judge his shortfalls and vulnerabilities. From now on, only God will see his failures. By putting away
the measuring tape, we can more freely watch our husbands grow.

**Needle and Thread:** These small items are a reminder of
how much easier it is to mend a torn shirt than a broken heart.
By putting these items in our box, we acknowledge the need to
place proper priority on our responses to unfortunate surprises
or accidents that caused us grief or loss. Every time I have react-
ed in anger over broken wedding china or mud tracks on a spot-
less floor, I end up grieving for the shattered sense of peace I
have brought on myself by lashing out.

**Tacks:** I use tacks to post reminder notes. Let these little
objects remind you to use tact, choosing the best time and place
to speak. "A word fitly spoken is like apples of gold in pictures of
silver" (Prov. 25:11, *KJV*).

**Glue:** We should endeavor by all means to "keep the unity of
the Spirit in the bond of peace" (Eph. 4:3, *KJV*). Just as glue
bonds, we must seek peace through unity. Peace is accomplished
by choosing to stick by what is right, not by who is right. Think
of glue as peace that you can carry around in your pocket and
apply when needed.

**Batteries:** Every woman needs an alternate source of energy.
We cannot blame others when we are not functioning properly
because our energy has been drained. Energy is drained when we
expect people to provide what only God can give us. We must make
time to recharge our batteries so that we can run on full speed.

## Questions to Consider

⊘ Which of these tools do you need to add to your relationship toolbox?

ꙅ What plans do you have to remind yourself not to use certain familiar tools?

ꙅ How will you record detailed instructions on how to use and apply these tools in your environment?

ꙅ How would you describe how to apply the bond of peace in your relationships?

ꙅ How can you save your energy for your closest relationships?

# Putting Your Words to Work

Now that we have covered the tools of the trade, let's take out our most powerful multipurpose tool—prayer. Through prayer your words become servants to the Spirit of God, sent forth to do the will of the Father. The best way to practice using this tool is to pray on paper and then to verbalize the written words in a free-flowing manner. Writing your prayers on paper reinforces a pattern of prayer and charts your requests. Just remember that you are not the architect, builder or supplier, but you are responsible to make your requests known to God.

Crying out to God is important; but just as a mother longs to hear thankfulness from her children, so our heavenly Father loves to hear our praise. I encourage you to spend time expressing your gratitude and praise to God.

Pattern your prayers after Philippians 4:6: "Don't worry about anything, but pray about everything. With thankful hearts offer up your prayers and requests to God."

ꙅ Father God, I am grateful for the investment You have made in me.

- ✒ I acknowledge the power that You have placed in my mouth.
- ✒ Let me be mindful of every word I release into the spirit realm.
- ✒ Give me Your desires, O God, that I may know what to prioritize in my prayers.
- ✒ Dear Lord, here are my requests. I make them known to You; accomplish Your will as You see fit.

Open your journal and make a honey-do list for the Holy Spirit. This list should comprise items of prayer that need your daily attention. As you incorporate your requests into your prayer time, keep your journal handy for writing down inspiration from the Holy Spirit. It is also extremely powerful to pray the Word of God. Not only will this be effective in reminding you of His Word, but it also is the primary way in which God will answer.

For married woman, this will be a reminder that it is unfair to require something of your husband that is the work of the Holy Spirit. For single women, the practice of turning your needs and your desires for security over to God will help you manage your expectations of your future marriage.

# CHAPTER 4

# TAKE A PEEK AT THE MASTER PLAN

*"For I know the plans I have for you," declares the LORD, "plans to prosper you and not to harm you, plans to give you hope and a future."*
JEREMIAH 29:11, *NIV*

I once saw in a shop window a pillow that read, "Love is blind, but marriage is a real eye-opener!" As funny as those words are, isn't it reassuring to know that we are not alone when it comes to experiencing the reality of marriage after the honeymoon? The words on the pillow may be an overstatement, but in today's world it seems as if it's a victory if the bride and groom are still smiling by the wedding day, let alone experiencing wedded bliss months later! No matter how you slice it, marriage isn't easy.

It should also comfort us to be reminded of Adam and Eve, who were placed in the middle of paradise, by the way. And did they have to mediate family fights or appease cranky in-laws in order to be together? No way! Yet their enjoyment was short-lived. In fact, like most of us, they had to face the cold, hard world of reality before their first child was born. Let's see what the Bible says about Adam and Eve's eye-opening experience.

> When the woman saw that the fruit of the tree was good for food and pleasing to the eye, and also desirable for gaining wisdom, she took some and ate it. She also gave some to her husband, who was with her, and he ate it. Then the eyes of both of them were opened, and they realized they were naked (Gen. 3:6-7, *NIV*).

## The Not-So-Perfect Beginning

I suppose it's possible that some marriages start with perfect beginnings, but most do not. I like to paraphrase Ecclesiastes 7:8 by saying that how we start out is far less important than how we end up. This seems to be true of marriage more than anything else, possibly because the damage done in the early years of marriage is often the reason that so many commitments end. We make mistakes that make us feel as though we will never recover.

To fully understand the institution of marriage, we have to go back to the beginning and review the tendencies passed down through previous generations. These iniquities, or leanings toward sin, are woven into our nature and played upon by demonic forces that desire our destruction, just as the weaknesses of Adam and Eve were targeted by the wickedness of the serpent. A lot can be learned from the dynamics of the fall of Adam and Eve. For now, I want to draw your attention to the part that Eve played in the scheme of things.

It wasn't an affair or a threat of divorce that brought trouble to paradise. It was a simple act of independence on Eve's part. She stepped out from under her husband's covering, and women the world over have been struggling with submission ever since. The only way to end this struggle is to restore the authority that was undermined through Eve's influence on Adam. Tragically, as a result of Eve's decision, Adam abdicated his position as head of their relationship and followed Eve's lead.

We must recognize the temptation to which Eve succumbed and reverse the act of deception that continues today: "And the serpent said to the woman, 'You will not surely die. For God knows that in the day you eat of it your *eyes will be opened*, and you will be like God, knowing good and evil' " (Gen. 3:5, *NKJV*, emphasis added).

## Lost in the Garden

The war against marriage began in the Garden of Eden. Let's dig up the past and discover the reasons why Satan desired to disqualify women as a voice of wisdom within marriage.

The first thing we lost in the Garden was our position as women and wives. Eve was deceived because she lacked revelation, not realizing that Satan was simply offering her what she already had. Then she was tricked into betrayal by the promise of becoming more like God through the intimate knowledge of good and evil.

Overthrowing authority was the first step Eve took toward intimately knowing evil. By severing her dependence on God, as well as her submission to her husband, she made her household vulnerable to the scheme of the Enemy. The serpent deceived Eve into believing that she would have a more powerful perspective if she yielded to his temptation. Yet all she brought on herself and her husband was the shame of being uncovered—naked and vulnerable. Their eyes were opened not to greater wisdom but to greater suffering.

It is true that throughout history women have suffered great injustices from efforts to silence and control them. I am grateful, as I'm sure you are, to enjoy certain rights that have come to us through the sacrifice of the women's suffrage movement. And yet a deep longing to restore a trust that cannot be mended by legislation and law still remains.

The second thing that happened in the Garden was that we lost our honor as woman—the latest and greatest creation. How could this deception have taken place if Eve had the revelation of who she was created to be? She was already made in the image of God, but she gambled away her future by succumbing to the serpent's promise of authority and greater knowledge and control. Eve may have been insecure in her role and thus vulnerable to attack. Our lives would be very different today if Eve had more fully known her role and had been more secure in her position. (Now, even in the most perfect environment, we deal with insecurity that can lead to stolen authority.)

Eve was the last creation of God and the first human casualty of sin. This knowledge alone should alert us that the enemy of God saw Eve as his foremost threat—and his easiest target. He didn't pick off God's creation in the order they were made; he went after woman first. Why?

Satan went after Eve because he knew that she was a pivotal player in the management of authority and obedience. Eve was chosen as a catalyst because of the power of her position and the influence she had with her husband. When Satan set out to deceive and displace Adam and Eve, he did not come to them with a sword drawn for battle. Instead, he covertly questioned their identity through everyday conversation. Today we are in a war with the same tempter who came to Eve. And every day he uses his most proven weapons against us.

When Satan singled out Eve for attack, he meant to tarnish her reputation and silence her for eternity. His goal was not only the failure of humankind through separation from God but also the breakdown of trust between a husband and a wife. After the Garden, how could a man ever truly know that a woman would not expose him to weakness and failure? After all, Eve's voice was used to dethrone Adam's authority, even as the serpent's voice was used to deceive her.

In the carnal mind of man, woman is often viewed as ignorant, gullible and easily deceived. This is part of the curse put on women after the Fall. I am not saying that every man acts according to this thought process, but there is an underlying ancient wound inflicted by Eve that remains today in the relationship between a man and a woman. The following is a revelatory quote on the makeup of a man from one of my favorite resources.

> You see, every man remembers Eve. We are haunted by her. And somehow we believe that if we could find her, get her back, then we'd also recover with her our own lost masculinity.[1]

Relationships with godly wives, mothers and sisters have restored many men's opinion of women. But we must recognize the damage of the past and take account of what was lost before true restoration can be achieved.

For the most part, the Enemy has succeeded in silencing the

voice of women for thousands of years. But we can overcome through the power God has put within the very pattern of our being. We simply have to recognize the flaws of our nature, identify the tricks of the enemy and give ourselves over to the spiritual revelation we possess.

You may not feel that you have any such revelation, but I will tell you this: You didn't put the revelation there, so you may not realize how deeply God has planted Himself within you. What women lost in the Garden can be restored through planting the seeds of repentance. These seeds take several forms. Praying the prayer of repentance is fundamental; then we change our ways as a result of the words of repentance we speak. The very direction of our lives and our destiny can be changed through the revelation of repentance.

## Putting Your Words to Work

Many believers see prayer as the opportunity to speak to God; but this is only one purpose of prayer. The real work being done while we pray is in us. We do not pray to bring God into agreement with us; we pray to set ourselves in submission to His will.

## Psalm 51: Pattern for the Prayer of Repentance

- Have mercy on me, O God,
- According to your unfailing love; according to your great compassion blot out my transgressions.
- Wash away all my iniquity and cleanse me from my sin.

- For I know my transgressions, and my sin is always before me.

- Against you, and you only have I sinned and done what is evil in your sight, so that you are proved right when you speak and justified when you judge.

- Create in me a pure heart, O God, and renew a steadfast spirit within me. Do not cast me from your presence or take your Holy Spirit from me. Restore to me the joy of your salvation and grant me a willing spirit, to sustain me (Ps. 51:1-4,10-12, *NIV*).

## Questions to Consider

- What is the first step I can take to participate in the restoration of the proper authority in my household?
- Why did Satan go after Eve first?
- Have my actions exposed my husband to vulnerability? If so, how?
- Have I been guilty of subtly overthrowing my husband's authority?
- What adds power to the prayer of repentance?

## What Comes After Wipeout?

Many people do not know how to clean the surface and begin again. Instead of immediately repenting, they resort to further destruction. We have all experienced disappointment in a relationship that can cause us to wipe out what we had built. Sometimes the betrayal we feel seems to outweigh the investment we have made. If you have done and said things you wish you hadn't, you are not alone.

There are places in a relationship that should be designated as out of bounds. If there are roads in your marriage relationship that you know are dead ends, then mark them as such and make the decision not to go down those roads again. Using the word "divorce" is one of those dead-end places. Unless you intend on driving your relationship off a cliff, guard your mind by setting boundaries.

The good news is that we don't need to experience cataclysmic destruction in order to begin again. In fact, we start over each time we choose repentance. The desire to start over comes from the feeling of failure we experience through trial and error.

Even God wanted an opportunity to start over! In spite of the evil of humankind and all the just reasons for the flood, God must have felt regret over the destruction of the world. It may help to know that God said, "Never again will the waters become a flood to destroy all life" (Gen. 9:15, *NIV*). Not only is it good to say, "I will never do that again," but it is also a declaration against destruction.

## Exercise: Declaration Against Destruction

Before we move on, now would be a great time to make your own declaration against destruction. A declaration is simply a written list of promises. Here is an example for married women: "It is destructive for me to remind my husband of the fact that I make more money than he does; therefore, I will never speak of this again. I recognize that this fact can be extremely hurtful to him. I will make a point of praising him for his contributions." An example for single women might be "I will never speak negative words over my future again. I will be consistent in my declaration of great things to come! My destiny is not dependent on the decisions of man; it is dependent on the plan of God."

This declaration should be a very personal one, so go as deeply and get as detailed as necessary to make your subconscious mind aware of your desire to change.

## The Preparation of Restoration

The quickest route to restoration is through submission. The first step we take in an act of submission is to face the brutal facts of our wrongdoing. If God can submit Himself to us, then we can surely submit ourselves to our husbands. They may not have it all together and be the spiritual leaders we feel that we deserve, but they are the God-ordained authorities in our lives. We will never see our husbands become all they were meant to be and what we've always dreamed of by lording over them. It is simply impossible to control or manipulate our husbands and have a healthy marriage.

We need to see ourselves as submitting to our husbands' needs as men. We can do great things to accommodate their deepest desires. We take care of them, and God will take care of us. Now you may be thinking, *Why do I have to submit first? If he is the spiritual leader, why doesn't he go first?* If you were thinking those thoughts—and I am not saying that you were, but *if* you were—the answer is simple: When your aim is restoration, then you need to take off layers in the order they were applied. When Eve participated with the serpent, she stepped out of line first, so it is our job as women to realign ourselves through submission first.

# What Is Submission?

I picture submission as a mission within a mission—smaller underlying tasks that, if assigned to me by God, I can control and that help in the accomplishment of a much larger goal (which is out of my control). Just as a submarine is in the ocean, under the surface, so we are in the will of God and under the covering of His plan when we submit. Submission takes many forms within marriage. I will never forget the way I learned the rewards of submission.

Let me set the stage by telling you that I married a man from Atlanta, Georgia, who loves homemade biscuits and lots of affection. In the first few years of our marriage, accommodating all of his little requests became overwhelming. We also had four children within three years, all before our fourth anniversary! This partially explains why I started to feel like I had another child when my husband would expect his biscuit to be buttered a certain way!

After long days of caring for three children in diapers (one set of twins), I had very few romantic feelings. But sure enough, when I would fall into bed for my hour or so of sleep before I would have to feed two babies, I had to make sure my husband was properly tucked into bed. It didn't take long before I told him that I couldn't be everyone's source of comfort, and that he was going to have to understand that I would rather say no to him than say yes and become bitter.

Not long afterward, God began dealing with me about my decision. When I prayed, I told the Lord that because of my lack of sleep I felt totally justified in laying down those rules. I had no help with the children and no help with the house. Did my husband expect me to die trying to please everyone? In that conversation, God promised me that if I would take care of my husband's needs, then He would take care of mine. And so, of course, I told the Lord that I would.

The very next morning there was a knock on the door. When I opened it, there stood a sweet woman I recognized from church. She said she lived down the street and told me that she had been asking God how she could be used during a season of her life that kept her home most of the day. She had felt led to offer to clean my house and help me with the babies. So you see, God was faithful to take care of me, but I had to *commit to submit* before I saw the fulfillment. God's way was much better than mine; He provided someone who brought restoration to my mind and body.

Unmarried women also need to practice their commitment to submit by serving others. Serving others can be done by mentoring other women, teaching Bible studies, hosting gatherings for other single women, and more. Don't limit the methods by which you will choose to serve. I wouldn't be preparing you for marriage if I didn't warn you that submitting to your future husband will require extreme flexibility. So you might as well start exercising those submission muscles!

## Combining the Practical and the Spiritual

This past year, my father found a little country chapel in a small town called Cross Roads, about an hour north of Dallas, Texas. He passed it regularly on his way north and noticed that it had been abandoned. When he explained his burden to buy the building, he said, "I just cannot stand the thought of an old church sitting among the weeds and being overtaken by lack of purpose."

Out of his love for nostalgia, he followed through with his mission to return the abandoned chapel to its original grandeur.

Layers of paint were removed, old carpet pulled up and the floor leveled and reinforced. The transformation process was so remarkable that people from the community began to ask a lot of questions about his plans for the little chapel.

During the physical restoration project, another transformation was in the works as well. Little did we know that God was simultaneously putting the finishing touches on the lives of the future pastors of Cross Roads Chapel.

During the three years prior to the chapel's renovation, a woman named Jenny was becoming weary with the singles' scene. As a pastor's daughter, she longed to be in the ministry but had endured years of disillusionment after her divorce. When her marriage ended, she felt as if God might never use her for the ministry as she had dreamed of since childhood. But God had a wonderful plan of restoration in the works. What Jenny didn't know was that a man named Randy, who had been one of her childhood friends, was at a similar place in his life. They were two single people waiting for the plan of God to unfold.

Toward the end of the restoration of the little chapel, things were speeding up for Randy and Jenny as well, beginning with a renewal of their long-lost relationship.

Not long after Randy and Jenny got reacquainted, they began dating. Within a short time it became clear to each of them that God had meant them for one another. Soon after they married, they felt the undeniable call to full-time ministry, but the role in which they would fulfill this dream was not yet apparent.

As the little Cross Roads Chapel was nearing completion, my father shared the progress with close family and friends. We were all so excited about how this chapel could potentially affect the surrounding area. As the possibility of the chapel's becoming a full-fledged church emerged, so did the possibility of Randy and

Jenny's becoming the pastors of Cross Roads Chapel. As God had ordained, the chapel was restored to a luster beyond its original creation. My father says that when he first saw the condition of the little chapel, he just knew it had to be fixed. I am sure that for a short time after he bought it, he questioned what all his hard work would bring. He never imagined that it would also be part of the restoration he had prayed for in the life of his sister—Jenny. Only God could so perfectly prepare a couple whose lives demonstrate restoration with a beautiful old chapel that was redeemed through a physical act of restoration.

Sometimes there are relationships in our lives that need restoration that only God can provide. We can hope and pray for God to do His best, but very often the natural need for restoration gives purpose to the spiritual transformation God is orchestrating on our behalf. All we can do is be obedient to fix what He places in our path and then watch Him work as He brings it all together at the crossroads.

God may not be calling you to restore an old landmark, but I am sure there are relationships in your life that could use a physical act of restoration. Acts of redemption take many forms: a phone call, a greeting card, an invitation to dinner, a favor bestowed or an errand run. The Word of God in action brings the power of redemption into our daily lives. How else can we demonstrate restoration except by using our lives for the purpose for which they have been restored?

When my father chose to pay for the restoration of an old building, he paid the price to buy back the building's purpose. Through repentance you pay the price for the restoration of relationship. It may not have been your actions that brought an end to the friendship, but it can be your actions that bring the redemption of it. I encourage you to pay the price for yourself and for others to experience the newness of restoration.

# A New Beginning

God did everything to make the Garden of Eden a place where Adam and Eve would love to dwell. Although God did tell Adam to tend the Garden, Adam and Eve began their life there with existing plants, not with barren, untilled land, as was the case after the curse. In the Garden, Adam and Eve's every need was supplied. All God asked of them was to fill the earth with people, bring the earth and its animals, fish and vegetation under control, and have communion with Him. There is no way they could have known how to appreciate what they had until it was too late. When God escorted Adam and Eve from the Garden, He didn't just release them—He also cursed the ground.

> Cursed is the ground because of you; through painful toil you will eat of it all the days of your life. It will produce thorns and thistles for you, and you will eat the plants of the field. By the sweat of your brow you will eat your food until you return to the ground (Gen. 3:17-19, *NIV*).

Not only did God refuse to be their gardener, but He also caused all circumstances to work against them. God made a new beginning with Noah when He said, "Never again will I curse the ground because of man. . . . As long as the earth endures, seedtime and harvest, cold and heat, summer and winter, day and night will never cease" (Gen. 8:21-22, *NIV*).

Then God spoke words He had not spoken since before the curse: "Be fruitful, and multiply, and replenish the earth" (9:1, *KJV*). God gave humankind a second chance to reap a different harvest. It didn't work when God did everything for Adam and Eve in the Garden, and it wasn't fruitful to strive in spite of a curse; so God instituted another plan for restoration. The new plan was to bless our investments—to combine His efforts with ours!

If we sow, He empowers the seed to produce. It is the best of both worlds. It is not all God or all man, but a joint effort of restoration based on sowing and reaping.

Restoration is a primary focus of life. We cannot paint pretty colors on big problems and hope they will get resolved. I look back and I don't know how our house or our marriage was still standing after the first several years. But God is faithful—and when we are faithful, and stick around, we see just how faithful He really is. He has the strength to sustain us through the greatest times of trial and testing.

Houses and furniture would not show age or wear if they were not used. If you are alive and have opinions, your relationships are going to get a little banged up now and then. So thank God for restoration. Live another day—patch another hole.

## Putting Your Words to Work

Pray for restoration, using these questions as a pattern:

- Are there neglected or destroyed areas of your life that could use restoration?
- What acts of restoration can you begin today?
- Have you left an argument hanging in the air?
- What is more important in the act of restoration—the person whom you love or the point that you are trying to make?

# Make a Declaration of Restoration

- ✍ What action will you take to signify your new beginning?
- ✍ How will you measure the restoration effort?
- ✍ What is your desired outcome?
- ✍ How would you describe your vision of complete restoration?

**Note**

1. John Eldredge, *Wild at Heart* (Nashville, TN: Thomas Nelson Publishers, 2001), p. 91.

PART 2

*Design Element:*

# UNITY

*The contrast of rugged and refined, of strong and gentle epitomize the fiery passion of romance. In robust country styles, delicate crystals hang from unadorned hand-forged iron chandeliers, and bronze farm roosters and rough stone are as appealing as cherubs and sculptures.*
BETTER HOMES AND GARDENS, ROMANTIC STYLE

The romantic style began in Rome, where a heavy stone lays behind a flowering herb. It is a decorating style that embraces contrast, and its essence is the unity between the extremely masculine and the fantastically feminine. This unique approach to decorating, which forms a cross-section of many styles united by the combination of male and female, produces a sense of comfort. Unity is not the loss of individual identity; it is the combination of contrast that makes a powerful vision indeed. Unity does not mean *bland*—it means *blend.* The romantic style works as a beautiful expression of unity in any design.

Romance in marriage functions much the same way by uniting a couple and their differences through affection and love.

My parents are what you would call opposites, and yet they appreciate many of the same decorative touches. I have seen them both admire the same object, but for different reasons. One of their most endearing knickknacks demonstrates this common ground. In my parents' first year of marriage, my mother went on a shopping spree for their first little house. While out looking for something special, she came across two alabaster dove figurines. The salesman told her a story about their practical use as well as their beauty. He explained that if the lady of the house is happy, she should turn the doves face-to-face. If she is upset at her husband, she should turn them back-to-back. After hearing his story, my mother thought she had an even better reason to buy them: They would be the perfect way to hint to my dad when he had done something wrong.

When my mother brought her treasure home, she took the birds out of the box and told my dad the story. After all, they wouldn't be useful if he didn't know how they worked. As it turned out, Dad loved those birds and the meaning they held, maybe even more than Mom did. To this day, he still tells the story of the "lovebirds" and shows them to people who visit my parents' house. My mother learned something valuable about my father that day: He loves anything that has a story behind it. So from that point on, Mom has shopped for his enjoyment as well as hers. It gives them something to share, and it helps make her house his home.

What about your home? Do you have any special decoration or accessory that represents both your and your husband's tastes? If not, find a way to purposefully incorporate your husband's favorite things into the design of a room.

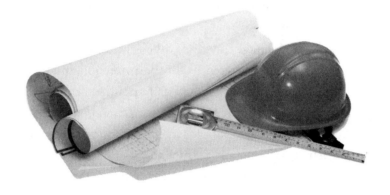

# CHAPTER 5

# ABRAHAM: THE MANTLE OF FAITH

*Now faith is the substance of things hoped for, the evidence of things not seen.*
HEBREWS 11:1, *KJV*

Abraham is often referred to as the father of faith. Abraham wasn't the only man in the Bible who demonstrated great faith, but he was the first man to forsake everything, even his family, to follow God. Although the Bible is full of stories about men and women of God who possessed great faith, there is something to say for being the first. And at that time, God was not known or understood in the vast way we experience Him today. Abraham had no written Word from which to learn about this God for whom he was risking all to serve. I am sure there were stories about the flood and the Tower of Babel that had been passed down, but these stories did not present the grace-covenant God we now know Him to be. Abraham forged an iron faith in the midst of heat and pressure. Each test that Abraham experienced had a purpose in making a broad, flexible, strong mantle for many nations to wear. Woven into his life were the threads of many ups and downs that made him a man of faith.

## Making the Mantle

In biblical times, a mantle, or cloak, was a garment worn over the shoulders. Each man's mantle was a symbol of his identity and authority; a mantle could be exchanged in the act of covenant making or passed down to his children as a symbol of his legacy and anointing. We are blessed to live in a time when the knowledge and anointing from men of the Bible can rest on us as a spiritual mantle. Let's follow the first thread of Abraham's mantle and see where it leads us.

Before Abram became Abraham, his first step of faith was to answer the call of God: "The LORD had said to Abram, 'Leave your country, your people and your father's household and go to the land I will show you'" (Gen. 12:1, *NIV*).

I am sure the first step of faith would have been easier if God had shown Abram where He would take him by giving him a map or directions. Leaving home and possessions behind may seem simple enough when we read about it in the Word of God, but we must realize that life doesn't happen as fluidly as one sentence flows to the next. God didn't make any promises of safety and security to Abram before requiring him to take action. Abram was prosperous and wealthy, living in a city of abundance, when God called him to separate from his father's house and travel until He told him to stop. I can hardly imagine how Abram explained this to his family!

Faith is the first step toward fulfilling the plan of God for our lives. Because faith is first, it is the most important step we take. All subsequent steps are meaningless if we are not willing to go the distance to experience true covenant with a God we know so little about.

Let's look at how Abraham exercised his faith. He proved that there was no limit to his faith. He may have had some ups and downs, but when he followed through with what God had asked of him and was prepared to sacrifice his only son, God knew that Abraham's value system and faith were in the right place. Abraham didn't put his faith in possessions. He didn't put his faith in geographical location or a piece of land. So where did Abraham put his faith?

Abraham proved that there was only one place to safely place his faith. He put his faith in God and in actions that carried out God's instructions. Some of Abraham's tests of faith required that he rely on God to fight his battles. For other tests, the only right answer was to engage his faith by taking action to fulfill the will of God. Each test was set in motion to prove Abraham's desire to know the perfect will of the God he loved. Here is a list of the tests Abraham endured.

- **The Test of Time:** Abraham could easily have lost faith many times while he waited for some sign of the fulfillment of God's promise to make him into a great nation (see Gen. 12:2).
- **The Test of Separation:** "The LORD had said to Abram, 'Leave your country, your people and your father's household and go to the land I will show you.' So Abram left, as the LORD had told him" (vv. 1,4, *NIV*).
- **The Test of the Tithe:** "Then Melchizedek king of Salem brought out bread and wine. He was priest of

God Most High, and he blessed Abram, saying,
'Blessed be Abram by God Most High, Creator of heaven and earth. And blessed be God Most High, who delivered your enemies into your hand.' Then Abram gave him a tenth of everything" (14:18-20, *NIV*).

☙ **The Test of Negotiation:** "Then the LORD said, 'The outcry against Sodom and Gomorrah is so great and their sin so grievous that I will go down and see if what they have done is as bad as the outcry that has reached me. If not, I will know.' Then Abraham approached him and said: 'Will you sweep away the righteous with the wicked? What if there are fifty righteous people in the city? Will you really sweep it away and not spare the place for the sake of the fifty righteous people in it? Far be it from you to do such a thing—to kill the righteous with the wicked, treating the righteous and the wicked alike. Far be it from you! Will not the Judge of all the earth do right?' The LORD said, 'If I find fifty righteous people in the city of Sodom, I will spare the whole place for their sake'" (18:20-21,23-26, *NIV*).

☙ **The Test of Circumcision:** " 'You are to undergo circumcision, and it will be the sign of the covenant between me and you. For the generations to come every male among you who is eight days old must be circumcised, including those born in your household.' On that very day Abraham took his son Ishmael and all those born in his household . . . and circumcised them, as God told him. Abraham and his son Ishmael were both circumcised on that same day'" (17:11-12,23,26, *NIV*).

Like Abraham's testing, our testing will take us to the place of faith where God's promises are confirmed and fulfilled. Exercising our faith is, in effect, putting a demand on the expectation we have of our creator to fulfill His promises. Not only do we replace our doubt with belief, but we also go beyond this to a place of complete expectation. Abraham approached God with utmost respect, but he didn't lose sight of who had made the promises in the first place. He continually reminded God that the promises were His idea, so they were His to perform. Abraham definitely had a handle on his role in the covenant process. He knew that his job was to receive the promise and believe the blessing—God would handle the rest.

## Missing the Mantle

Abraham was most vulnerable when it came to relationships. On several occasions his vulnerability resulted in fear regarding his wife's beauty. Two different times Abraham pretended that Sarah wasn't his wife in order to protect his life. Although he was hiding behind Sarah, he wasn't completely lying when he claimed that she was his sister, since they shared the same father. Therefore, she was his half sister as well as his wife. This scenario may seem strange to us, but it was very common for husbands to be killed so that a covetous man could possess another man's wife.

Poor Abraham. Like most men, he could pass almost every test God threw at him, but he couldn't get past the situation with his wife. In addition, when Sarah, who was barren, encouraged Abraham to sleep with her maidservant, which resulted in the birth of Ishmael, she also made him vulnerable to the fear that God would not come through and produce the promised seed through Sarah. After waiting many years, Sarah must have given in to feelings of guilt over not having produced an heir and her sense of obligation to do so. How could Abraham have said no to her when, at that time, a woman's worth was tied to her ability to bear children? So Abraham agreed to Sarah's plan, but there was trouble with it from the word "go"!

> He slept with Hagar, and she conceived. When she knew that she was pregnant, she began to despise her mistress [Sarah]. Then Sarai [Sarah] said to Abram, "You are responsible for the wrong I am suffering. I put my maid-servant in your arms, and now that she knows she is pregnant, she despises me. May the LORD judge between you and me" (Gen. 16:4-5, *NIV*).

After Hagar ran from Sarah, she later returned with the blessing of God. This awkward scenario worsened as her son, Ishmael, grew and her resentment smoldered. Both Hagar and Ishmael were a constant irritation to Sarah, and eventually they were sent away. The sadness of this ancient struggle continues today; the descendants of Isaac and Ishmael are at war with one another and have been for centuries—and it all began with fear. Sarah's lack of faith caused her to jump ahead of God's timing and create her own disaster—and Abraham played right into her hands. The situation probably would have been easier for Sarah if God had forgotten Ishmael altogether instead of giving him a blessing. Under God's hand of blessing, even our mistakes have lives of their own.

## Modeling the Mantle

Abraham's ultimate test:

Some time later God tested Abraham. He said to him,

"Abraham!" "Here I am," he replied. Then God said, "Take your son, your only son, Isaac, whom you love, and go to the region of Moriah. Sacrifice him there as a burnt offering on one of the mountains I will tell you about" (22:1-2, *NIV*).

Abraham laid his son Isaac upon an altar to prove the faithfulness and goodness of God. To trust God with his promised son, Isaac, was the most challenging test that Abraham ever faced. Abraham's actions have come to define the very meaning of faith. From his life we learn that faith is not only belief, but it is also the ability to trust the One in whom we believe.

Isaac was the embodiment of everything God had promised to Abraham. We know that Abraham was wise and that he knew that God needed his son to build a nation from his body. (God had already told Abraham that Ishmael was not the heir from whom all nations would be blessed.) Yet Abraham didn't flinch or need a moment to decide if he would follow through with God's request. He immediately took action—through obedience—to show his trust in the Lord. This instantaneous response was the model of faith set for us by Abraham.

Early the next morning Abraham got up and saddled his donkey. When they reached the place where God had told him about, Abraham built an altar there and arranged the wood on it. He bound his son Isaac and laid him on the altar, on top of the wood. The he reached out his hand and took the knife to slay his son. But the angel of the LORD called out to him from heaven. (vv. 3,9-11, *NIV*).

Many Christians do not know what to think about a God who would make such a request. They may even wonder if God would ever ask something similar of them. Or maybe they wonder why God would test us at all if He already knows our thoughts and intentions. I believe that many people are bothered by Abraham's experience but haven't put their finger on why. What is the purpose of testing in our lives? Does God need proof of our faith? If so, why?

God asks for proof of our faith by requiring corresponding action. Although He already knows our thoughts and intentions, He also knows that we have one major flaw: Our actions do not always line up with our intentions. So the testing of trust is meant to prove that we can lay all of our faith on the line and follow through with our side of our covenant with God.

A covenant is a binding agreement to share all pain and possession with the one with whom we are in covenant. We have to remember that God made a covenant with a human being who could not give back anything but faith. Abraham, like all humans, had nothing else to offer a God who had created all things. The only thing any of us can hand over to God is our will, and then we take on His will through trust. With Abraham, God went first when it came to fulfilling His part of the promise; then Abraham performed the only way he could demonstrate his part of the covenant—he placed Isaac on the altar.

## Questions to Consider

- ⚿ What did Abraham's test of trust prove?
- ⚿ Do you think Abraham passed the test of time, or did he make his own plan?
- ⚿ How can you exercise your faith?
- ⚿ Have you ever passed a great test of faith? If so, how?

# Authority at a Glance

Wearing the mantle of faith means that

- ✍ you live as if the fulfillment of the promise has already taken place;
- ✍ you may be required to leave a place of prosperity to pursue your relationship with God;
- ✍ you are already practicing the first step toward fulfilling God's plan for your life;
- ✍ you will be tested in the context of your closest relationships.

# Pattern for Prayer

- ✍ Father, I thank You for giving me insight on faith.
- ✍ Show me how to build my faith, and keep me from destruction that comes through fear.
- ✍ I acknowledge the fruit of faith in the life of Abraham, and I ask to receive a double portion of his anointing.
- ✍ I am willing to walk in submission to Your will.
- ✍ Let my life demonstrate Your power of transformation and impartation as I endeavor to encourage my husband's faith.
- ✍ By Your Spirit, Lord, lay on my husband and my household Your mantle of faith. May faith forever rule our lives.

# Declarations

- ✍ I will choose to take God's view of my husband.

⚘ I will see my husband wearing the mantle of Abraham.

⚘ I will affirm my husband's calling to walk by faith.

⚘ I will uphold my role by restoring my husband's authority.

⚘ I will encourage him by building him up.

## Seal It with a Gift

This section, here and throughout the book, is designed to engage your action through generosity. A gift is a concrete way to declare the reality of your husband's mantle—God's impartation of his identity and authority. By purchasing something for yourself, or for you and your husband (as my mother purchased the lovebirds for my father so many years ago), you can place small reminders in your home that represent the transformation you are undergoing.

The gift of vision represents the mantle of faith. Listed below are some recommended gifts. Anything with a lens that processes an image will do. Be creative as you think of something with vision to buy for your husband. You might want to get something for yourself as well. His and hers sunglasses would be a great gift for both of you!

⚘ Sunglasses

⚘ Glasses

⚘ Binoculars

⚘ Telescope

⚘ Camera

# Isaac: The Mantle of Obedience

*He learned obedience by the things which He suffered.*
HEBREWS 5:8, *NKJV*

My family is notorious for starting projects without reading the instructions. From model airplanes to new Christmas toys, we just don't consult the directions very often. I think this trait makes life a little more adventurous for us! One year, when my brother was about three years old, he begged my father to put his new toy together. After my father agreed, Stephen quickly said, "Where's the destructions, Daddy?"

We all laughed at his little word mix-up and the irony of his question, because our plans to assemble a project always seemed to head for destruction when we failed to consult the instructions.

# Making the Mantle

Isaac seems better known for the actions of others *toward* him rather than for his own actions. He was raised in the shadow of a mighty father who had great wealth and influence. And then he fathered a child he named Jacob, who later became known as Israel. The better-known facts of Isaac's life make him look like a victim: placed as a sacrifice on the altar by his father, Abraham; and then tricked into giving the firstborn son's right of blessing to Jacob, his second son. But before we downplay Isaac's legacy with the well-known facts, let's examine the value of what Isaac brought to the table.

In the beginning, Isaac brought great joy to his parents. In fact, his name means "God has made me laugh." He was the fulfillment of God's promise to Abraham many years before. Not only did Isaac personify the covenant relationship between God and man, but he also demonstrated the resolution of Abraham's trust in God through the sacrifice of obedience.

> Then God said, "Take your son, your only son, Isaac, whom you love, and go to the region of Moriah. Sacrifice him there as a burnt offering on one of the mountains I will tell you about." Isaac spoke up and said to his father Abraham, "Father?" "Yes, my son?" Abraham replied. "The fire and wood are here," Isaac said, "but where is the lamb for the burnt offering?" Abraham answered, "God himself will provide the lamb for the burnt offering, my son." And the two of them went on together. When they reached the place God had told him about, Abraham built an altar there and arranged the wood on it. He bound his son Isaac and laid him on the altar, on top of the wood. Then he reached out his hand and took

the knife to slay his son. But the angel of the LORD called out to him from heaven, "Abraham! Abraham!" "Here I am" he replied. "Do not lay a hand on the boy," he said. "Do not do anything to him. Now I know that you fear God, because you have not withheld from me your son, your only son" (Gen. 22:2,7-12, *NIV*).

When we think about the story of Abraham's taking Isaac to the mountain with every intention of sacrificing him, how many of us would ever put ourselves in Isaac's place? Although most of us would say that we have learned obedience the hard way, our stories wouldn't hold a candle to Isaac's. I must admit, I have rarely considered Isaac's point of view. When I have, I usually think of him as a child who had no choice but to obey. But Isaac was young and strong, while his father was old and distressed by what he must do. I venture to guess that if Isaac had wanted to rebel against his father, he easily could have run away. Yet he was obedient to his father, even in the face of death. He didn't disobey and run away, although no one would have blamed him if he had. Although Isaac experienced the pressure of becoming the sacrifice of his father's faith, whether he obeyed was a test of his own faith as well.

I may not have been able to trust God or man after such a traumatic event, but Isaac never wavered from his father's ways of worship. This experience may have been just the thing to introduce Isaac to a healthy fear of the Lord. He willingly laid his life on an altar as a young man; this same method of laying down his life followed him throughout his life in the form of obedience.

## Missing the Mantle

In most chapters of this book, the "Missing the Mantle" section will explore a vulnerability faced by the man being profiled and will showcase it as a potential area of weakness. With Isaac, we are going to take this section a slightly different direction, primarily because the very nature of obedience makes its owner vulnerable, placing him at the mercy of someone else's—in this case, God's—actions. Through obedience the point of exposure is orchestrated by God to ultimately bring those who wear this mantle closer to Him.

Our obedience to God is the act of laying down our lives to His will. With every decision to obey, we are transformed by the nature of God created within us. Because of its power to transform, obedience is perhaps the most necessary yet underrated virtue in a child of God.

So why do we hold other attributes in higher esteem? Perhaps because obedience is not a tool that makes us feel more powerful; in fact, the more we practice obedience, the more vulnerable we become.

If to obey means that we follow instructions without negotiation or delay, then there is no room for our exerting control or manipulation. The very essence of obedience may be why many theologians see passivity in Isaac's nature. It is a sad reckoning when a boy is thought to have had no ideas of his own when he acts according to his father's wishes.

Another reason that obedience is such a vital tool in our transformation is because of its two-sided quality. When we give our allegiance to God by obeying his Word, we are vulnerable to Him in every way. This vulnerability doesn't weaken us. Instead, we are aligned with the perfect will of God, which makes us powerful in the eyes of our enemies. We are invincible when we are dispatched in the army of God, wearing a mantle of obedience.

Because of Isaac's formidability, we see little or no deviation from his job during his reign as head of the family. He fulfilled his commission to multiply and take possession through the act of obedience.

## Modeling the Mantle

Obedience is the bridge that makes the impossible possible. We see this kind of obedience put in action in the life of Isaac.

> Now there was a famine in the land—besides the earlier famine of Abraham's time—and Isaac went to Abimelech king of the Philistines in Gerar. The LORD appeared to Isaac and said, "Do not go down to Egypt; live in the land where I tell you to live. Stay in this land for a while, and I will be with you and will bless you. For to you and your descendants I will give all these lands and will confirm the oath I swore to your father Abraham. I will make your descendants as numerous as the stars in the sky and will give them all these lands, and through your offspring all nations on earth will be blessed, because Abraham obeyed me and kept my requirements, my commands, my decrees and my laws." So Isaac stayed in Gerar (26:1-6, NIV).

We often give credit to the pioneers of a certain movement or event while overlooking the faithful men and women who come after and maintain growth through consistency. Isaac was a bridge of obedience that stretched from one generation to another, linking the legacy of Abraham to his offspring. Consistent obedience is not easy to do. It would be especially difficult to be asked to stay put during a time of famine.

Isaac planted crops in that land and the same year reaped a hundredfold, because the LORD blessed him. The man became rich, and his wealth continued to grow until he became very wealthy. He had so many flocks and herds and servants that the Philistines envied him. So all the wells that his father's servants had dug in the time of his father Abraham, the Philistines stopped up, filling them with earth (vv. 12-15, *NIV*).

By these Scriptures, it becomes very clear that Isaac was blessed for his obedience. He had the choice to disobey God and go in search of prosperity, but instead he chose to stay, and God blessed him, in spite of the current famine. This prosperity is what eventually pushed Isaac out from among others.

Then Abimelech said to Isaac, "Move away from us; you have become too powerful for us." So Isaac moved away from there and encamped in the Valley of Gerar and settled there. Isaac reopened the wells that had been dug in the time of his father Abraham (vv. 16-18, *NIV*).

To maintain the blessing God put on his father, Abraham, Isaac was called to restore wells and reinstate vows as a representative of a new generation. Because Isaac was the model of blessing due to his obedience, his enemies desired peace with him and his household.

This is the declaration of Isaac's enemies, who sent him away in anger:

Isaac asked them, "Why have you come to me, since you were hostile and sent me away?" They answered, "We saw clearly that the LORD was with you; so we said, 'There ought to be a sworn agreement between us'—between us and you. Let us make a treaty with you that you will do us no harm, just as we did not molest you but always treated you well and sent you away in peace. And now you are blessed by the LORD' " (vv. 27-29, *NIV*).

Although Isaac had not been sent away in peace, his enemies surely desired to rewrite history by pursuing him to make peace. Isaac's obedience brought a blessing to him that caused his enemies to fear the Lord!

## Questions to Consider

- Why do we hold some attributes in higher regard than obedience?
- Why do women struggle with the temptation to be independent?
- Has your future been at stake while someone else's faith was being tested? How so?
- Do you find it difficult to follow directions without knowing all of the details?
- In what ways have you laid down your life to God?
- Have the same struggles followed your family from generation to generation?
- How can godly fear help restore honor to your husband and others in authority over you?

## Authority at a Glance

Wearing the mantle of obedience means that

ঌ you are living in a manner that is more important to God than sacrifice;

ঌ you will be required to lay down your life in many areas;

ঌ your calling requires vulnerability;

ঌ your lifestyle can move your enemies to desire peace with you.

## Pattern for Prayer

ঌ Father, I thank You for giving me an appreciation for obedience.

ঌ Show me how to build my trust in You, and keep me from the destruction that comes through disobedience.

ঌ I acknowledge the fruit of obedience in the life of Isaac, and I ask to receive a double portion of his anointing.

ঌ I willingly walk in submission to Your will.

ঌ Let my life demonstrate Your power of transformation and impartation as I endeavor to encourage my husband's choice to obey your Word.

ঌ By Your Spirit, Lord, lay on my husband and my household Your mantle of obedience. May obedience forever rule our lives.

## Declarations

ঌ I will choose to take God's view of my husband.

ঌ I will see my husband wearing the mantle of Isaac.

- I will affirm my husband's calling to walk by obedience.
- I will uphold my role by restoring my husband's authority.
- I will encourage my husband by building him up.

## Seal It with a Gift

Because obedience is like a death that produces fruit, perhaps planting a seed to grow a plant is the best concrete declaration of the mantle of obedience. I suggest that you purchase gardening supplies for at least one plant. You could also buy a plant, but it is great fun to sprout seedlings yourself. This exercise will require that you follow directions, create a healthy environment for the plant and give it daily attention. I think you will find that there is a wide variety of flower and herb seeds available. Check the back of seed packets for the calendar growth schedule and ideal locations to be sure that you leave the store with a viable plant project. When your plant begins to flourish, you will have a tangible reminder of your declaration to live in obedience to God in your home and through your actions.

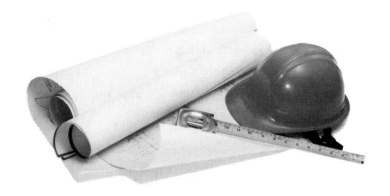

# CHAPTER 7

# JACOB: THE MANTLE OF DETERMINATION

*Set your affection on things above, not on things on the earth.*
COLOSSIANS 3:2, *KJV*

Determination is neither a good nor bad quality. How determination is used makes it good or bad. If a person is determined to please God and sets his or her mind on doing so, then determination is good. If determination causes a person to lie, cheat or steal in order to manipulate blessing, then determination is bad.

In the life of Jacob, determination played a big role in making him who he was. During the early years of his life, Jacob used his gift of determination to manipulate his circumstances in pursuit of his own selfish desires. Later we see that God showed Jacob how it feels to be taken advantage of. This experience ultimately led to Jacob's change of heart—his very nature and eventually his name change. Jacob's life is a wonderful example of how natural gifting can be misguided and misused and then redeemed for the purpose God intended.

# Making the Mantle

Jacob's name means "supplanter," which means to uproot or take from. This name was given to him at birth, because even then he was working to manipulate his rank.

> After this, his brother came out, with his hand grasping Esau's heel; so he was named Jacob (Gen. 25:26, *NIV*).

What began as a birth-order issue eventually led Jacob to desire the power and the standing of the firstborn son. Not only was Jacob the second-born son, but he was also second choice as his father's favorite. Jacob was not the outdoorsman that Esau, his older brother, was. Apparently this fact gave him less favor in the eyes of his father, Isaac, from whom the firstborn birthright and blessing were bestowed. And above all, Jacob desired that blessing. He soon found an opportunity to manipulate his circumstances and supplant his brother.

One day while Jacob was cooking, Esau approached him with a need. Esau was very hungry and wanted to eat some of the food Jacob was preparing. This was Jacob's chance to use what he had to get what he wanted.

> Jacob replied, "Sell me your rights as the first-born son."

"I'm about to die," Esau answered. "What good will those rights do me?" But Jacob said, "Promise me your birthrights, here and now!" And that's what Esau did. Jacob then gave Esau some bread and some of the bean stew, and when Esau had finished eating and drinking, he just got up and left, showing how little he thought of his rights as the first-born (vv. 31-34).

The birthright had been transferred to Jacob; now all he needed was the blessing. Jacob was his mother's favorite, and she had always looked out for him. In this case, she was listening for him as well. Together, Rebecca and Jacob plotted to deceive Isaac, who was old and nearly blind, into blessing his second-born son (see 27:1-29). Jacob accomplished this deception by dressing in Esau's clothing. Although Isaac questioned Jacob's quickness and the sound of his voice, Isaac's suspicions were appeased by touching Jacob's clothing. So Isaac blessed Jacob instead of his firstborn, Esau.

Later, when Isaac realized what had happened, he was very upset by the deception; but the blessing had already been given and could not be reversed. Esau begged his father to bless him also, but little was left for him. When Isaac responded to Esau by saying, "Indeed he shall be blessed," (v. 33, *NKJV*), Esau cried, "Is he not rightly named Jacob? . . . He took away my birthright, and now look, he has taken away my blessing!" (v. 36, *NKJV*).

Esau threatened to kill Jacob, so Rebecca got Isaac to send Jacob away to find a wife from among her family. Jacob was sent away from everyone he knew because of his trickery. He had not realized that his determination to have it all would eventually force him out of his own family. As Jacob found out, manipulation often results in isolation.

# Missing the Mantle

Jacob was most vulnerable to familiar devices and methods. By using determination to deceive, Jacob entered a cycle by which he would also become a victim of someone else's manipulation. Jacob was deceived in a most vulnerable area—love. When he asked for Rachel's hand in marriage, Rachel's father, Laban, gave Jacob a taste of his own medicine. Although an agreement had been reached in the purchase of Rachel as Jacob's wife, Laban deceived Jacob and gave him his other daughter, Leah.

I can well imagine that Jacob knew immediately that he deserved to be deceived, but that didn't change the fact that he wanted Rachel. So he agreed to work seven more years for her. After he purchased both wives, Jacob entered negotiations to separate from Laban. Jacob wanted to go back to the place of his birth and take his family with him. What should have been a simple transaction turned into another of Laban's tricks. After God had seen the faithfulness of Jacob in spite of Laban, He blessed Jacob and gave him a plan to prosper from Laban's flocks. When Jacob had had enough of trickery, he left without Laban's knowledge.

# Modeling the Mantle

After years of doing things the wrong way, Jacob was determined to make things right. He diligently pursued the right path by seeking out his brother, Esau.

And Jacob told them to be sure to say that he was right behind them. Jacob hoped the gifts would make Esau friendly, so Esau would be glad to see him when they met. Jacob's men took the gifts on ahead of him, but he spent the night in camp. Jacob got up in the middle of the night and took his wives, his eleven children, and everything he owned across to the other side of the Jabbok River for safety. Afterwards, Jacob went back and spent the rest of the night alone (32:20-24).

Then he addressed changing himself.

A man came and fought with Jacob until just before daybreak. When the man saw that he could not win, he struck Jacob on the hip and threw it out of joint. They kept on wrestling until the man said, "Let go of me! It is almost daylight!" "You can't go until you bless me," Jacob replied. Then the man asked, "What is your name?" "Jacob," he answered. The man said, "Your name will no longer be Jacob. You have wrestled with God and with men, and you have won. That's why your name will be Israel" (vv. 24-28).

Jacob's determination took a right turn when he determined that he would rather die than stay the same and keep his old nature. He wrestled with the angel of the Lord and would not let go until he was changed. Even when Esau declined Jacob's gift of reconciliation, Jacob was determined that Esau would receive from him.

When determination is focused only on selfish gain, it is a destroyer; but when determination is aimed at the pursuit of God and His will, it redeems. Jacob was not released from his years of manipulation until he had wrestled for a change in his name and his nature. The mantle of determination was a powerful connecting force in the life and lineage of Jacob, who became Israel.

# Questions to Consider

- In what areas do you lack determination? In what areas does your husband lack determination?
- Have you struggled with manipulation? How?
- Is it easier for you to manipulate than to wait?
- Has manipulation ever isolated you from someone you love? How so?
- How can determination connect you to God's purpose in your life?

# Authority at a Glance

Wearing the mantle of determination means that

- you must work hard to avoid selfish desires that could drive you to manipulate circumstances;
- your mantle may isolate you from others;
- you are able to persevere and not give up a struggle until change occurs;
- you will have many opportunities to understand that a changed nature is more important than a change in circumstances.

# Pattern for Prayer

- Father, I thank You for giving me insight regarding determination.
- Show me how to build my determination, and keep me from the destruction that comes through apathy.

- I acknowledge the fruit of determination in the life of Jacob, and I ask to receive a double portion of his anointing.
- I willingly walk in submission to Your will.
- Let my life demonstrate Your power of transformation and impartation as I endeavor to encourage my husband's determination.
- By Your Spirit, Lord, lay on my husband and my household Your mantle of determination. May the pursuit of Your will forever rule our lives.

## Declarations

- I will choose to take God's view of my husband.
- I will see my husband wearing the mantle of Jacob.
- I will affirm my husband's calling to walk in determination.
- I will restore my husband's authority by choosing not to manipulate him.
- I will encourage him by working *for* him, not *against* him.

## Seal It with a Gift

Like determination, tools are neutral until we put them to work either in building or destroying. The power in the tool is harnessed when it is used for the purpose for which it was made. So for this demonstration, I suggest that you buy your husband a specialty tool (or a tool set if he doesn't already have one). But don't give him a honey-do list right away! If your husband already has enough tools but has a hard time finding them, I suggest gathering the tools and organizing a man domain for him in the garage.

Cooking utensils wouldn't be a bad investment either. Most women could use a little help in the kitchen.

Gift suggestions:

- Power tools
- Toolbox for storage
- Gift certificate to a hardware store
- Cooking utensils

# Unity by Design

*Unity is the combining or joining of separate things or entities into one; it is the harmony of opinion, interest or feeling.*

**Design goal:** To unify your home's design theme.

There are many important unifying treatments in home design. However, none of these can compare to the unification among the inhabitants (which make up the home) and the house itself. The designer must make a conscious effort to bring cohesion to the space while at the same time making everyone feel at home.

Most of us do not live in a Tuscan farmhouse, in a Swiss chalet or in a Montana log cabin, so decorating themes may be a bit more elusive for us to identify. This becomes especially challenging in America, where we have a mixture of cultures.

Perhaps the driving force behind the theme of your home's design should be the interests of those who live there. As you answer the following questions, look for broad themes that could combine your family's common interests and also inspire spiritual awareness.

- Does your home reflect the personality of your family?
- What interests each person living in your home? What does he or she feel passionate about or dream of doing one day?
- Does your home openly display those interests, passions and dreams?
- Does your family have a dream or mission that you share in common or would enjoy completing together?

⌗ What are some creative ways that you could integrate those interests into your home decor?

Here are suggestions that have a domino design effect.

⌗ Music: Frame sheet music or use it as wallpaper; hang old records as wall art; display musical instruments.

⌗ World Missions/Travel: Frame maps or use them as wallpaper; frame foreign money and travel posters; display old suitcases.

⌗ Movies: Hang large framed posters, film reels, old cameras.

⌗ Comics and Toys: Use comic books as a border; frame vintage comics; display vintage toys of famous collections.

Here are some tips to help unify your home:

1. Bring the outdoors inside, and the inside outdoors. To bring nature inside, use plants in the kitchen and bathroom; hang outdoor iron elements inside (on the wall); set up a water fountain inside. On outside patios or porches, set up usable living space with colorful pillows and patterns that bring indoor comfort outside.

2. Combine masculine and feminine elements. Make sure each room in your home has both strong and soft elements. This combination is very inviting.

3. Colors and styles will flow if they are complementary, not compartmentalized. Try using different value combinations of the same colors throughout your house—lighter colors in the entryway and exterior

rooms and deeper colors in the interior rooms. Each room has a primary emphasis color that may only be an accent color in the other rooms; using a touch of every other hue gives congruency to the visual flow of your home. You don't want your rooms to announce themselves as different from the rest of the house by color only. People should notice the color based upon the feeling of comfort or cheer the color gives them. I categorize my colors based upon the moods I like to perpetuate in that space. For instance, I want my kitchen to be cheery, so I always go with a bright or warm color like golden yellow. A bedroom should be restful, so cooler shades should be used. Although I love red, it is a color that demands response, so it is best used in an office, kitchen, game or media room.

4. Take all knickknacks to the kitchen table and redistribute them in different rooms. You will be surprised to find that something you specifically bought for a certain room will be the perfect spice for another place in your home. Don't limit your choice of which knickknacks you redistribute. When you look from a brown room into a purple room, you want to see splashes of purple accents in the brown room as an introduction or segue to the next room.

PART 3

*Design Element:*

# CREATIVITY

*Create in me a clean heart, O God; and renew a right spirit within me.*
PSALM 51:10, *KJV*

*It takes great passion and great energy to do anything creative.*
AGNES DeMILLE

I have always wondered why people think it is all right to say they are not creative. This proclamation bothers me especially when spoken by believers. Admitting that we have not created is one thing, but to adamantly diminish our mission to be like God is another. God *is* creativity, and He has made us in His image and likeness. Therefore, claiming to lack creativity is essentially claiming a lack of the presence of the Creator.

Creativity is not to make something out of nothing (only God can do that). Creativity brings existing things together to give them a new, improved function and style. Just remember, we are a combination of mud, water and the breath of life. God then created individuals by mixing a completely new recipe of DNA for each of us to put His unique stamp on our form. He didn't stop creating after six days; every moment of our lives He is making new things spring forth. When God creates, He looks at His creation and says, "This is good!" You, too, need to know the feelings of creating and appreciating your design. It is a fundamental way to be like our Father and to accomplish His commission to *replenish* the earth.

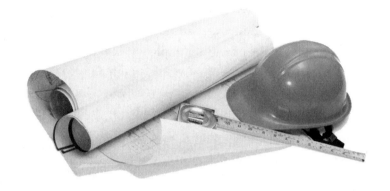

CHAPTER 8

# JOSEPH: THE MANTLE OF DREAMS

*Go confidently in the direction of your dreams.*
*Live the life you have imagined.*
HENRY DAVID THOREAU

Dreams are vivid and bold, like young Joseph's coat of many colors. Dreams can come to us as the result of favor and, without warning, make us the target of others' hatred and jealousy. If you have been labeled a dreamer, it most likely hasn't come about because you've had only one dream. Dreamers are called such because they have many visions of things to come. Often there is a stigma attached to the mantle of dreamer that causes the bearer to suffer for his or her dreams. How do we keep our dreams alive in the midst of discouragement? How do we hold on to integrity even when it means that we may lose our identity? Let's take a closer look at the dreamer's mantle to see if a pattern emerges.

# Making the Mantle

Joseph wore many mantles throughout his lifetime. Each of his garments, or cloaks, was a symbol of his favor and authority. He started with a coat of many colors, a gift from his father, Jacob. In those days the common way to dye a garment was to dip the whole thing in one color. Common colors came from the earthy tones of the desert. It was rare to see a garment made from various colored fabrics that were woven together. Joseph's garment must have been very costly and very beautiful in comparison with most mantles.

> Now Israel loved Joseph more than any of his other sons, because he had been born to him in his old age; and he made a richly ornamented robe for him. (Gen. 37:3, *NIV*).

This multicolored robe came to represent Joseph's role as the favored in the family. Seeing his son wear the robe must have made his father even more proud than he already was. Joseph's brothers, however, were jealous of the increasing identity Joseph had as the favored son.

> When his brothers saw that their father loved him more than any of them, they hated him and could not speak a kind word to him (v. 4, *NIV*).

More than likely, Jacob's other sons felt rejected and yearned for favor to disprove their feelings of inferiority. Is it possible that Leah's sons also bore the rejection of their mother? After all, she was fully aware that Jacob preferred Rachel, the wife of his heart, and spent most of his nights with her. Dan, Naphtali, Gad and Asher were the sons of Rachel and Leah's maidservants, which made these particular sons even lower on the totem pole of power. These boys carried an additional offense against Joseph when he tattled on them:

> Joseph, a young man of seventeen, was tending the flocks with his brothers, the sons of Bilhah and the sons of Zilpah, his father's wives, and he brought their father a bad report about them (v. 2, *NIV*).

Although Joseph wasn't perfect, even at a young age he upset the system by showing integrity. He may have been immature in the manner of his actions, but one thing is clear: Joseph was not a pleaser of men. With favor and integrity on his side, all Joseph needed to become the leader of the family was a vision. His high standards, combined with his father's favor, united his brothers in offense against him. The trap was set.

> Joseph had a dream, and when he told it to his brothers, they hated him all the more. He said to them, "Listen to this dream I had: We were binding sheaves of grain out in the field when suddenly my sheaf rose and stood upright, while your sheaves gathered around mine and bowed down to it." His brothers said to him, "Do you intend to reign over us? Will you actually rule us?" And they hated him all the more because of his dream and what he had said (vv. 5-8, *NIV*).

As we can tell from the text, Joseph's dream debut didn't go over so well. His tell-it-like-it-is way of communicating didn't show sensitivity on his part. But his first experience didn't stop him from trying to convey his second dream.

Then he had another dream, and he told it to his brothers. "Listen," he said, "I had another dream, and this time the sun and moon and eleven stars were bowing down to me." When he told his father as well as his brothers, his father rebuked him and said, "What is this dream you had? Will your mother and I and your brothers actually come and bow down to the ground before you?" His brothers were jealous of him, but his father kept the matter in mind (vv. 9-11, *NIV*).

Joseph had a childlike boldness when he spoke of this dream to his father and brothers. As a parent, his father rebuked his son for his seeming arrogance. His father must have feared the anger of his other sons but underestimated their level of hatred and resentment. Little did Jacob know that his sons were plotting Joseph's death when he sent Joseph to check up on them.

But they saw him in the distance, and before he reached them, they plotted to kill him. "Here comes that dreamer!" they said to each other. "Come now, let's kill him and throw him into one of these cisterns and say that a ferocious animal devoured him. Then we'll see what comes of his dreams" (vv. 18-20, *NIV*).

Reuben, the oldest of the brothers, begged the others to spare Joseph's life, convincing them instead to throw him into the cistern rather than shed his blood.

## Missing the Mantle

When were Joseph's dreams ripped away from him?

> So when Joseph came to his brothers, they stripped him of his robe—the richly ornamented robe he was wearing—and they took him and threw him into the cistern (vv. 23-24, *NIV*).

It is ironic that Joseph's brothers took the multicolored robe before doing anything to him. They wanted to possess the favor and position that was represented in the mantle. Joseph was disrobed and thus dishonored for a period of time on two separate occasions. The first attack, brought on by his brothers, was meant to displace and discourage his dreams. The second attack was on his character, when he refused to sleep with Potiphar's wife. She tore his robe from his body and exposed him to false accusations when he wouldn't abuse his authority through compromise (see Gen. 39).

Although favor exposed Joseph to attack and vulnerability, we can see that he knew his value beyond the title he carried, as represented by his robe. Joseph was diligent to earn and keep his authority in Potiphar's home the right way. He reminded the mistress of the house of all he was lord over and where the boundaries were set.

> "With me in charge," he told her, "my master does not concern himself with anything in the house; everything he owns he has entrusted to my care. No one is greater in this house than I am. My master has withheld nothing from me except you, because you are his wife. How then could I do such a wicked thing and sin against God?" (39:8-9, *NIV*).

Potiphar's wife wouldn't stop her pursuit of Joseph despite his efforts to ignore her. One day, when no one else was in the house, she "caught him by his cloak" ( v. 12, *NIV*) and demanded that he grant her wish. Instead, he left his cloak in her hand and ran from the house.

The fact that Joseph fled the situation in such a way shows us some very important things about his character. He obviously had a great fear of God, which caused him to flee temptation: "How then could I do such a wicked thing and sin against God?" he told Potiphar's wife. There is another interesting element of evidence here—his cloak. With no regard for the consequences to his authority or title, he traded his cloak for freedom. He preferred prison to a palace, if living in luxury meant losing his integrity. So after being stripped of his mantle for the second time, he was sent to prison. In the life of Joseph, we can clearly see how others' jealousy made him vulnerable or caused him to be uncovered—literally and metaphorically.

## Modeling the Mantle

Joseph used his God-given gift of interpretation to fill in the blanks for others' dreams long before he saw his own dreams fulfilled. It's interesting that we don't see Joseph striving to make his dreams reality. Throughout his life he had no control over his position, but in every situation in which he found himself— son, slave, prisoner—he experienced elevation. We might look at his life and think, *He had no choice; he was a slave.* But we need to look closer. Somewhere along the line, Joseph decided to be a diligent dreamer. The level of elevation given to him in every role shows us that he chose to add to his abilities in preparation for the big picture.

God always gives us opportunities to be diligently trained in the areas of our dreams. Those dreamers who suffer great discouragement over each setback are the ones who do not diligently apply their dreams to everyday opportunities. I believe that Joseph's greatest model for us today is the integrity with which he preserved his dreams. When we read the account of his time in prison, we see that he found favor once again, this time in the eyes of the warden.

Joseph's dreams developed in the dungeon. He put his gift to use by interpreting the baker's and the cupbearer's dreams in the palace prison (see Gen. 40). The baker's dream foretold his own death; the cupbearer's dream foretold his own reinstatement to the king's favor. The cupbearer, who was indeed freed and restored to his position, seemed to have forgotten Joseph's service to him until God gave Pharaoh a dream that needed an explanation. Then Joseph was quickly brought before the ruler. Joseph's interpretation of Pharaoh's dream was that seven years of abundance would be followed by seven years of famine. Not only did Joseph have the gift of interpretation, which he exercised in prison, but he also had instruction for Pharaoh based on his past experience in diligently managing Potiphar's household.

It is interesting to note that Joseph experienced firsthand what it felt like to go from feasts in Potiphar's house to famine in a prison cell. What he learned through the downsizing of his own position gave him the wisdom to instruct Pharaoh on the best course of action for the preservation of Egypt. Not only would his diligence set up a country that would sustain many other nations as well as his own, but it would also give him the platform to preserve the children of Israel as they grew in number.

Although Joseph had worn the multicolored mantle as a boy, he would model the prefix "multi-" as a man. Through his seasons as a servant, vizier and prison guard, he gained the skills and abilities needed to fill a multifaceted position. Although Joseph wore a new robe every time he took on a new role, we finally see him modeling the mantle of his dreams.

> Then Pharaoh said to Joseph, "Since God has made all this known to you, there is no one so discerning and wise as you. You shall be in charge of my palace, and all my people are to submit to your orders. Only with respect to the throne will I be greater than you." So Pharaoh said to Joseph, "I hereby put you in charge of the whole land of Egypt." Then Pharaoh took his signet ring from his finger and put it on Joseph's finger. He dressed him in robes of fine linen and put a gold chain around his neck (41:39-42, *NIV*).

In the end, Joseph lived many years and was able to see his father and his brothers live in prosperity under his authority and protection. Now, didn't we see that coming?

## Questions to Consider

- What would handling your dreams with integrity look like?
- Up to this point, have your efforts to make your dreams happen generated personal cost to your reputation?
- Do you have a plan for prioritizing and preserving your dreams during times of persecution?
- Have your high standards ever seemed to put your dreams in a holding cell?
- How do you think you would prepare for seasons of

famine while you are experiencing great abundance?

✍ In your life, are there dream thieves whom you need to release by forgiving them?

# Authority at a Glance

Wearing the mantle of a dreamer means that

✍ you will have to choose integrity over identity;

✍ you are empowered through experience before you are anointed with authority;

✍ you will come to understand that the feelings and actions of others (whether positive or negative) are out of your control;

✍ you may receive favor that exposes you to the jealousy of others;

✍ you will experience promotion to a higher level of authority—in spite of difficult circumstances—if you maintain integrity in the way you live.

# Pattern for Prayer

Use the answers to your questions above as a pattern for prayer.

✍ Begin by thanking God for giving you dreams.

✍ Repent for lost or abandoned dreams.

✍ Pray for the revival and fulfillment of your dreams.

✍ List your dreams and your husband's dreams separately.

# Declarations

- ✍ I will choose to take on God's view of my husband.
- ✍ I will see my husband wearing the mantle of Joseph.
- ✍ I will affirm my husband's calling to dream big.
- ✍ I will uphold my role by restoring my husband's authority.
- ✍ I will encourage my husband by building him up.

# Seal It with a Gift

To encourage the heart of a dreamer, here are some gift suggestions that go with the dream theme:

- ✍ Monogrammed pillow
- ✍ Pajamas
- ✍ Robe and slippers

I would enjoy buying these items for myself, especially silk pajamas! Who says the single girls get to keep all the good stuff!

When I originally prayed the mantle of Joseph over my husband, I went with the coat-of-many-colors theme by taking him to buy a new suit. Use your imagination to create the perfect gift for your husband!

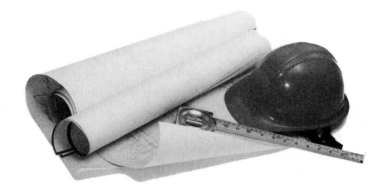

# CHAPTER 9

# MOSES: THE MANTLE OF COMMUNICATION

*Let my words and my thoughts be pleasing to you, LORD.*
PSALM 19:14

Moses, an Israelite, was raised in the house of Pharaoh. He was trained in the royal Egyptian academy and was given all the luxuries a prince should receive. It is said that he spoke four or more languages by the age of 12. Moses' first stage of life with the Egyptians gave him a foundation of knowledge that God would later use for His glory.

# Making the Mantle

The circumstances in which Moses left his season at the palace probably erased in his own mind all of his qualifications for power and authority. His life as a prince came to a close very quickly. When he ran from his crime of murder, he was driven into the desert and lived there 40 years before God called out to him from the burning bush.

> One day, Moses was taking care of the sheep and goats of his father-in-law Jethro, the priest of Midian, and Moses decided to lead them across the desert to Sinai, the holy mountain. There an angel of the LORD appeared to him from a burning bush. Moses saw that the bush was on fire, but it was not burning up. "This is strange!" he said to himself. "I'll go over and see why the bush isn't burning up." When the LORD saw Moses coming near the bush, he called him by name, and Moses answered, "Here I am." God replied, "Don't come any closer. Take off your sandals—the ground where you are standing is holy. I am the God who was worshiped by your ancestors Abraham, Isaac, and Jacob." Moses was afraid to look at God, and so he hid his face.
>
> The LORD said: "I have seen how my people are suffering as slaves in Egypt, and I have heard them beg for my help because of the way they are being mistreated. I feel sorry for them, and I have come down to rescue them from the Egyptians. I will bring my people out of Egypt into a country where there is good land, rich with milk and honey. I will give them the land where the Canaanites, Hittites, Amorites, Perizzites, Hivites, and

Jebusites now live. My people have begged for my help, and I have seen how cruel the Egyptians are to them" (Exod. 3:1-9).

In verse 11, Moses questioned his own identity when he asked, "Who am I to go to the king and lead your people out of Egypt?" The combination of the two very different lives that Moses had led may have left him without a sense of identity and feeling very insignificant and out of sync. After 40 years of living in the desert, his people skills were a bit rusty. What a difference to spend the first half of your life in a palace and the second half in a desert wilderness! But God's ability to use Moses was not affected by Moses' lack of self-identity; God saw Moses as a deliverer. This should be a lesson to all of us. If God calls us, it is not our identity that matters; the only thing that matters is that God is with us.

[And God said:] "Now go to the king! I am sending you to lead my people out of his country."

But Moses said, "Who am I to go to the king and lead your people out of Egypt?" God replied, "I will be with you. And you will know that I am the one who sent you, when you worship me on this mountain after you have led my people out of Egypt." Moses answered, "I will tell the people of Israel that the God their ancestors worshiped has sent me to them. But what should I say, if they ask me your name?"

God said to Moses: "I am the eternal God. So tell them that the LORD, whose name is 'I Am,' has sent you. This is my name forever, and it is the name that people must use from now on" (vv. 10-15).

After Moses questioned his own capability, he then questioned God's as well. If he was going to be sent on behalf of God, he certainly needed to know who God was. The reply Moses received reflected the history of God with His people and the covenant, which required God to deliver them from suffering. The Bible says that God was moved by the cries of His people. God needed *someone* to say, "Let my people go!" He needed a deliverer, and he chose Moses.

After Moses led the people to freedom, he began to learn even more about the God of his forefathers. Moses became the single most important communication link between God and man. As his leadership duties expanded, Moses became weary with the pull of communicating with the people. So his father-in-law, Jethro, made a wise observation.

> Jethro replied: "That isn't the best way to do it. You and the people who come to you will soon be worn out. The job is too much for one person; you can't do it alone. God will help you if you follow my advice. You should be the one to speak to God for the people" (18:17-19).

By advising Moses to spend the majority of his time with God instead of man, Jethro showed great wisdom. It seems obvious that one would desire God's presence more than answering the demands of others—even if the demands are urgent. But what Moses' situation shows us is that our feelings of responsibility can overshadow our calling to communicate with God. Spending quality time with God is always a great investment. This is especially true when there are things that God needs to impart through us, which was the case with Moses. Once Moses began to seek intimate communication with God, many structures came into form for the children of Israel.

# Missing the Mantle

If the gift of communication was only having something to say, then Moses would have had it made. So why was he reluctant? Because there is another important ingredient in effective communication—confidence. This is where Moses was most vulnerable; he lacked confidence. He judged his own hesitation and fear as a deficit when it came to speaking in public.

Just because we are called to be communicators doesn't mean that we are free from fear when we need to communicate. Moses demonstrated in a strong way that our greatest fears can become the areas in which God will choose to use us. Moses' story teaches us that when it comes to communication, opportunity is greater than ability.

> Moses replied, "I have never been a good speaker. I wasn't one before you spoke to me, and I'm not one now. I am slow at speaking, and I can never think of what to say." But the LORD answered, "Who makes people able to speak or makes them deaf or unable to speak? Who gives them sight or makes them blind? Don't you know that I am the one who does these things? Now go! When you speak, I will be with you and give you the words to say." Moses begged, " LORD, please send someone else to do it."
>
> The LORD became irritated with Moses and said: "What about your brother Aaron, the Levite? I know he is a good speaker. He is already on his way here to visit you, and he will be happy to see you again. Aaron will speak to the people for you, and you will be like me, telling Aaron what to say. I will be with both of you as you speak, and I will tell each of you what to do" (4:10-16).

Moses' hesitation angered God, but He honored Moses' request to make Aaron the spokesman to the people. However, God would not speak to Aaron directly. In effect, God was saying that Aaron would only be empowered to say those things that Moses was inspired to communicate to him. Moses was the anointed prophet, and God did not want to work around His chosen plan.

I believe that God compromised His perfect will to accommodate Moses until he was comfortable probably because Moses made a suggestion, not a refusal. Although Moses must have experienced fear over his lack of ability, I sense that his real desire was for God to be represented with excellence—a noble request. But the truth is, even the most eloquent speaker could not have softened Pharaoh's heart.

God continued to stretch Moses' communication skills by requiring new things of him. When God changed the method of releasing water from striking a rock to verbally commanding the water, Moses reverted. His lack of confidence ultimately led him to miss out on the culmination of his life's work.

> And [God] said, "Moses, get your walking stick. Then you and Aaron call the people together and command that rock to give you water. That's how you will provide water for the people of Israel and their livestock." Moses obeyed and took his stick from the sacred tent. After he and Aaron had gathered the people around the rock, he said, "Look, you rebellious people, and you will see water flow from this rock!" He raised his stick in the air and struck the rock two times. At once, water gushed from the rock, and the people and their livestock had water to drink. But the LORD said to Moses and Aaron, "Because you refused to believe in my

power, these people did not respect me. And so, you will not be the ones to lead them into the land I have promised" (Num. 20:7-12).

When God instructed Moses, He commanded him to *speak* to the rock instead of striking the rock with the rod, as he had on a previous occasion. We don't know why Moses chose to disobey and do it the old way, but I suspect his deviation was due to the method God used. God told him to *speak* to the rock. It seems that the change God communicated to Moses and Aaron was a way of stretching Moses' leadership, not just testing his listening skills. The resulting punishment when Moses disobeyed had lasting effects on Moses' legacy as the leader of the children of Israel.

## Modeling the Mantle

Moses' greatest contributions to the kingdom of God were his writings and implementation of worship and godly living through the canon of Scripture called the Pentateuch—the first five books of the Bible. The divine communication that Moses experienced with God revealed the history of creation and humankind in the book of Genesis. In Exodus, Moses kept an account of all the experiences of the children of Israel that occurred under his leadership. In Leviticus we learn about the process and implementation of the priesthood, the construction of the Tabernacle and the Law. The book of Numbers chronicles the processes of counting the children of Israel and of mapping territory. Deuteronomy is perhaps best described as a recap of all that happened under the leadership of Moses and also is a declaration over the future of Israel.

# Questions to Consider

- Are you a gifted communicator or a hesitant speaker? How about your husband?
- Have you ever seen your husband respond to an injustice or a great need by breaking through his comfort level of communication?
- Do you see yourself as a mouthpiece for your husband, as Aaron was for Moses?
- What form of communication comes more naturally for your husband: writing or speaking?

# Authority at a Glance

Wearing the mantle of communication means that

- you will be given opportunities to be God's spokesperson;
- you will find that God works *with* your weaknesses, not *around* them;
- you can fulfill your mission without perfect execution of the details;
- you may not be allowed to enter an area of God's blessing if you do not accurately follow God's instructions and accurately communicate His message to others;
- you must work at eliminating distractions that keep you from the ultimate communication opportunity—prayer.

# Pattern for Prayer

Using your answers above, pray over your husband as a communicator. Pray that his strengths will be fruitful and used by God, and that his weaknesses will develop into strengths. Pray for his confidence and for the purpose behind his words. Pray that God will send him an overriding purpose that will draw him toward clearer communication.

- Father, I thank You for the gift of quality communication.
- Show me how to build my communication skills, and keep me from destruction that comes through confusion.
- I acknowledge the fruit of communication in the life of Moses, and I ask to receive a double portion of his anointing.
- I willingly walk in submission to Your will.
- Let my life demonstrate your power of transformation and impartation as I endeavor to encourage my husband's communication.
- By Your Spirit, Lord, lay on my husband and my household Your mantle of communication. May Your Word forever rule our lives.

# Declaration

- I will choose to take on God's view of my husband.
- I will see my husband wearing the mantle of Moses.
- I will affirm my husband's calling to higher communication.

- I will uphold my role by restoring my husband's authority.
- I will encourage my husband by building him up.

## Seal It with a Gift

Any tools of communication would be good for this mantle. My husband is a computer guy, so I would buy him "computer stuff," but the basics are always appreciated.

- A fine writing pen
- A letter opener
- Desk or stationery set

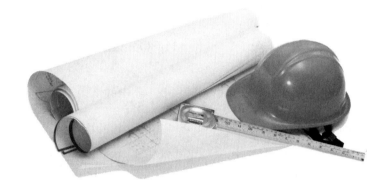

# JOSHUA: THE MANTLE OF SUBMISSION

*Submission is the only good;*
*Let me become an instrument sharply stringed*
*For all things to strike music as they please.*
PHILIP LARKIN

When you know that you are well equipped to be a leader and accomplish things on your own, it can feel counterproductive to lay down your abilities to become a servant. Yet the ability to submit—to make a humble entrance into the lives of others—is a quality possessed by the greatest leaders.

Submission leads to insight, knowledge, relationship and unity. The catch is that first we must become servants before we can enjoy submission's benefits. Submission requires that we serve others and get our hands dirty, with no promise for advancement. The true spirit of a person is revealed when he or she is forced to choose between submission and what would appear to be a more desirable opportunity.

My mother has a great analogy for submission. When she once asked the Lord to show her how He views submission, He reminded her of one of her own experiences. As she pictured this memory of nursing her child, a question came to mind: Who is more submitted, the mother or the baby? As she considered her answer, she came to the conclusion that the mother walks in a deeper level of submission than the child. The baby has no other choice but to lie there and receive from its mother; the mother, however, must choose to lay down her life, putting everything else on hold in order to meet the needs of her baby. She is walking in a greater level of submission because of what she sacrifices to serve her child.

My first tests of submission began when I was learning to obey my parents. When it was time to make my own decisions, I could have chosen to gradually tune out my parents' advice. The older I became, the less rebellious it would have seemed to move ahead with no care for the opinions of others. But this is the stage when submission starts to become a noticeable sacrifice.

After I married and had children of my own, I realized that submission was the only path to contentment. If I fought the boundaries of my situation as a wife and mother, I would lose the joy of fulfilling those wonderful roles. Submission is the opposite of doing what we can; it is *the action of doing what is most beneficial for our lives and our relationships.*

Joshua was a man who modeled submission through many sacrifices, which ultimately led to his leadership of the Israelites. Although he could have accomplished much on his own, instead he humbly chose to assist Moses. His unassuming faithfulness quickly got him noticed by both God and man.

## Making the Mantle

Joshua first distinguished himself as a leader during the Israelites' initial battle. Moses depended on Joshua to defend the children of Israel and later to scout out their future in Canaan. Joshua and Caleb are best known for bringing back a good and confident report of what was in the land. The reports from the other scouts were negative and reflected fear and doubt. Joshua and Caleb's focus was not on their enemies but on their God-given destinies.

> And Caleb stilled the people before Moses, and said, Let us go up at once, and possess it; for we are well able to overcome it (Num. 13:30, *KJV*).

Although Joshua returned to Moses with great excitement about taking the land, he had to submit to the fact that everyone didn't have his kind of faith. Joshua must have been quite disheartened to realize that he was not surrounded by others who possessed the same belief in God and in themselves. But Joshua knew that if he was going to lead the people, then he had to return to where they were, stay with them until they matured and then bring them into the land. This was a huge test of submission. Imagine the difficulty of knowing what they could have possessed and yet accepting that they were not ready. The maturation of the younger generation and the dying off of the older generation took more than 40 years. In the meantime, Joshua served Moses and submitted himself to training.

# Missing the Mantle

Similar to obedience, submission creates vulnerability. This vulnerability increases when the level of leadership increases. Just when you think you have a few battles under your belt and you are feeling the victory, you get hit with a more concentrated form of submission. Each test builds on the last battle. Joshua knew battle; he had fought and won many of them. Although he was known as a warrior, his role as the spiritual leader of the children of Israel was just beginning, and this was a prime time for him to be tested.

In Joshua 7:1, after the victory in Jericho, Joshua sent scouts to Ai. In verses 2-5, the children of Israel (not knowing about Achan's rebellion) went to battle against Ai and were defeated. When Joshua asked God why they had lost this battle, the Lord said:

> Stop lying there on the ground! Get up! I said everything in Jericho belonged to me and had to be destroyed. But the Israelites have kept some of the things for themselves. They stole from me and hid what they took. Then they lied about it. What they stole was supposed to be destroyed, and now Israel itself must be destroyed. I cannot help you anymore until you do exactly what I have said. That's why Israel turns and runs from its enemies instead of standing up to them (vv. 10-12).

God then told Israel exactly what He desired them to do to rectify their relationship to Him (see vv. 13-15, *KJV*).

- Destroy the accursed thing from among you.
- Sanctify the people.

⌀ Bring the people up according to their tribes.

⌀ When the accursed thing is found, it shall be burnt by fire.

So Joshua did as God commanded, and it soon became obvious that the guilty party would not confess willingly. God would have to point him out. First God revealed the tribe, then the family, then the actual household and finally the man, Achan.

"Achan," Joshua said, "the LORD God of Israel has decided that you are guilty. Is this true? Tell me what you did, and don't try to hide anything." "It's true," Achan answered. "I sinned and disobeyed the LORD God of Israel. While we were in Jericho, I saw a beautiful Babylonian robe, two hundred pieces of silver, and a gold bar that weighed the same as fifty pieces of gold. I wanted them for myself, so I took them. I dug a hole under my tent and hid the silver, the gold, and the robe." Joshua had some people run to Achan's tent, where they found the silver, the gold, and the robe. They brought them back and put them in front of the sacred chest, so Joshua and the rest of the Israelites could see them. Then everyone took Achan and the things he had stolen to Trouble Valley. They also took along his sons and daughters, his cattle, donkeys, and sheep, his tent, and everything else that belonged to him. Joshua said, "Achan, you caused us a lot of trouble. Now the LORD is paying you back with the same kind of trouble." The people of Israel then stoned to death Achan and his family. They made a fire and burned the bodies, together with what Achan had stolen, and all his possessions (vv. 19-25).

After experiencing one of the most glorious victories imaginable, Joshua was subjected to loss because of one man's lack of submission. Joshua himself was fully submitted to the authority of God, but he was also subject to the obedience of the people. God instituted this system of checks and balances to keep leaders in touch with their people. As the Israelites' leader, Joshua was vulnerable to suffer the consequences of their rebellion.

This vulnerability was clearly demonstrated through Israel's most humiliating loss under Joshua's leadership. By allowing the Israelites to lose in spite of the odds in their favor, God was teaching them submission and showing them that each individual carried the burden of obedience for everyone else. This meant that if one walked in rebellion against the command of God, then everyone would suffer defeat.

We can be obedient without being totally submitted, but we cannot be submitted without being totally obedient. Submission is a position of accountability in which we willingly place ourselves. The difference between obedience and submission is that submission is a lifestyle, not a one-time action.

## Modeling the Mantle

All of Joshua's battles speak of submission. In the battle of Jericho, Joshua submitted to a rather unconventional way of laying siege by following God's instructions. As a result, he experienced great victory and honor.

The LORD was helping the Israelites defeat the Amorites that day. So about noon, Joshua prayed to the LORD loud enough for the Israelites to hear: "Our LORD, make the sun stop in the sky over Gibeon, and the moon stand still over Aijalon Valley." So the sun and the moon stopped and stood still until Israel defeated its enemies. This poem can be found in *The Book of Jashar.* The sun stood still and didn't go down for about a whole day. Never before and never since has the LORD done anything like that for someone who prayed. The LORD was really fighting for Israel (10:12-14).

How powerfully this story illustrates submission! Joshua's dedication to the will of God had been so fully demonstrated that he knew God's will and commanded that it be done. For the battle to be won, Joshua needed the sun to remain in the sky until utter defeat had come upon their enemies. Submission drew Joshua so close to God that he knew what God wanted, and his request was for God to make His will possible. A request such as this could only have been demanded from someone whose motives had been measured by submission. God would not take suggestions from someone who had not been walking in submission. But God literally moved heaven and Earth to answer the prayer of a submitted man.

## Questions to Consider

Let these questions guide your prayer of repentance and restoration.

- With what submission issues have you battled?
- When have you chosen submission?
- How did God reward you for your choice?
- What have you taken that may make you a target for destruction?

- Can you name ways that your husband submits to you?
- Have you fought battles that God would have fought for you if you had submitted to His timing?
- Have you ever shown a lack of submission by speaking against an authority in your life?
- Has someone else's lack of submission caused you suffering or loss? How?

## Authority at a Glance

Wearing the mantle of submission means that

- you model faith in the face of doubt;
- you will lay down your ability to make your own future;
- your submission is a lifestyle that grows out of your consistent decision to obey;
- your level of submission can literally cause God to move heaven and Earth for your sake.

## Pattern for Prayer

- Father, I thank You for giving me insight into submission.
- Show me how to apply submission, and keep me from destruction that comes through stolen authority.
- I acknowledge the fruit of submission in the life of Joshua, and I ask to receive a double portion of his anointing.

- ✍ I willingly walk in submission to Your will.
- ✍ Let my life demonstrate Your power of transformation and impartation as I endeavor to encourage my husband in submission.
- ✍ By Your Spirit, Lord, lay on my husband and my household Your mantle of submission. May submission forever rule our lives.

# Declarations

All declarations are to be spoken aloud. Unlike the declarations in previous chapters, this particular declaration should begin with you, whether you are single or married. For those of you who are married, after you have spoken the declarations of your submission aloud, you can tailor the words to declare the mantle of submission for your husband as well.

- ✍ I will wear the mantle of submission.
- ✍ I will sacrifice even when I have the choice to do otherwise.
- ✍ I will give my will over to the plan of God for a greater cause.
- ✍ I will serve under my husband's and God's authority and receive impartation.
- ✍ I will wage war in the Spirit, bringing down the prosperity of the Enemy.
- ✍ Through submission, I will lead many to inherit God's promises to them.
- ✍ I am becoming a woman of God who walks in authority because I wear the mantle of submission.

&#8753; I will pray that my husband will be empowered to walk in the spirit of Joshua.

## Seal It with a Gift

The best gift to demonstrate submission involves a heart—primarily because that is where submission begins.

My suggestion for this demonstration is the gift of a special occasion planned by you for your husband. To intimately give yourself without reservation is the greatest act of submission. Why not create an evening of delight that encompasses his favorite things? You can begin by leaving a series of notes and surprises throughout the day, all leading up to an unforgettable evening—restaurant and romance included. The best part for him will be your creativity and thoughtfulness, both of which go a very long way with a man. The submission message is very accurately given by enjoying an activity he loves yet knows you aren't fond of.

To purchase a memento that represents submission, I suggest a decorative heart or cross accessory.

&#8753; Wind chime
&#8753; Bookmark
&#8753; Jewelry

# Creativity by Design

*Creativity can be as simple as using something for a completely new purpose. The main thing is to think outside of the box.*

**Design goal:** To use your gift of creativity

These are some of the best ideas I have seen for using existing items in creative ways. I hope they inspire you to try them for yourself; or use them as ideas to come up with your own variations!

1.  Picket-fence headboard for a bed: Picket fence is sold in small sections at home-improvement stores. You can purchase a new one and paint it; or for an aged look, check salvage yards or flea markets.
2.  Old denim jeans for curtains: One of my best friends made these curtains for her son's bedroom. It's just too cute and so simple to make. For a short valance, cut the jeans at thigh length and then from top to bottom along one of the side seams. Next, run a curtain rod through the belt loops and hang the valance! You can use as many pairs of jeans as needed to cover the top of a window. You can also make a dust ruffle by using these same instructions but running a rope or bandana through the belt loops and then tying all bandanas' ends together. The bandanas on each end would be tied to the bed rail, bedpost or bed frame.
3.  Family art gallery: Ask your children to paint pictures, and have them matted and framed for the family room and bathrooms.

4.  Linoleum rug: When you have small children, kitchen rugs are usually an inconvenience or they quickly become worn. Buy a 6x9-foot piece of linoleum sold on the roll for about $15. Paint a base color over the linoleum, and then use your creativity to make your own design. You can create a border with black checks or stripes and have your children make their handprints for the design. Stars and swirls can add a whimsical flair, but the trick is in the imperfection. Don't even try to outline perfectly. After you have painted your rug, sign it and then use a brown stain as a glaze. You simply wipe on stain in circular motions and wipe off with a dry rag. Let your creation sit overnight, and then spray it with a clear coat of polyurethane to seal. These rugs are wonderful ways to incorporate a favorite saying or quote. They are colorful and can be easily cleaned. Small pieces of linoleum can be painted to match your rug and used for placemats. After you create your rug, you may say to yourself, *Forget putting this work of art on the floor,* and end up using it as a wall hanging (use a rod with metal clips, if you do).

5.  One-of-a-kind photo artwork: Use the computer or a photo-cropping service to create one-of-a-kind artwork using candid snapshots. Using your favorite pictures, zoom in on the face of each member of your family and create a separate photo image. The photos don't have to have a common theme to pack a big punch, but unique facial expressions are my favorite—a child pouting or covered in baby food, or even the family pet! Use a close-up of your husband in action—fishing, swimming, golfing or otherwise.

The pictures can be printed in black and white or sepia to bring unity to the images. Next, you will need to pair each picture with a mat and frame. Before framing, have each family member decorate his or her own mat. (You choose the colors of paint ahead of time to be sure they are complementary.) Babies can add their personal touch with handprints and footprints.

I once decorated our kids' bathroom in a bubble theme. I scoured my collection of pictures and gathered every picture of my kids in the water—bathing or swimming. I resized the photos (when necessary) and cut each picture into the shape of a circle. I placed my favorite pictures in round frames and hung in a meandering line (resembling floating bubbles), and all the others were used in a wire picture holder that fans out from a base.

*Design Element:*

# AUTHENTICITY

*A pine table is a proper thing, but a pine table that pretends
to be black walnut is an abomination.*
ELLA RODMAN CHURCH

*Surely you desire truth in the inner parts; you teach me
wisdom in the inmost place.*
PSALM 51:6, *NIV*

I see a tragic trend in decorating today. Many couples go to a
popular furniture store and buy all new furniture and accessories to replicate a look they have seen in a catalog. In the
process, they throw out their history—anything from their past
that doesn't go with the new look. Every time the trend changes,
they throw out the "old" and buy all new stuff to keep their look
up-to-date. The only place for a room without history is in a catalog that becomes history when the new catalog comes out!

When we are obsessed with keeping up with trends lest we get caught in a time warp, we do not adequately reflect the depth of our life stages and experiences. Holding on to the living history of our homes—precious treasures kept in special places that remind us where we have come from and what we love—allows us to be authentic. There's something to be treasured from every era in our lives. A room without history is as dissatisfying as people who hide their identities and experiences.

Don't cover up your history; it is the proof of your progress. Many people have no lingering sense of legacy, simply because their past did not seem to complement their future. Because of either mistakes or shame of family background, they have erased the past in search of the future. We all need to guard against falling into that trap, and we can do so by being real and transparent about every layer of who we are.

Fine buildings continue to be destroyed for parking lots, highways, apartments, office buildings, and motels. But people are beginning to object. They are searching for their roots, something to build on, something in which they can take pride. Young people, particularly, are reacting against the plastic society, the emptiness, lack of character, solidity of suburbia, and the sameness of apartments and developments. They are coming back into the cities to find, under layers of filth, the fine homes their ancestors deserted decades ago. They are peeling back the linoleum from parquet floors, releasing mahogany shutters and sliding doors that were nailed up into walls when capricious fashion shunned them, stripping caked enamel off carved woodwork and bronze hardware, and repairing insets of etched and stained glass. Some of these young people are taking great pains to restore carefully and authentically. It is a labor of love and pride.[1]

**Note**

1. Deidre Stanforth, *Restored America* (New York: Praeger, 1975), p. 15.

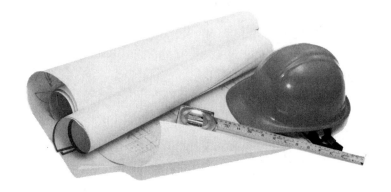

# CHAPTER 11

# SAMUEL: THE MANTLE OF DEDICATION

*I ask only one thing, LORD: Let me live in your house every day of my life to see how wonderful you are and to pray in your temple.*
PSALM 27:4

To be capable of heartfelt dedication is an attribute every woman would desire in her husband. You want to feel that he is faithful to you out of passion and desire and not out of obligation or lack of a more promising opportunity. It is no mystery that God would desire the same, if not greater, level of devotion from us. Few individuals have truly been separated for service unto God in the way that Samuel was. His story demonstrates this virtue in action.

# Making the Mantle

Samuel, who served as high priest of Israel during a season of transition, is most remembered for his entrance into the world through the prayers of his mother, Hannah. She was one of two wives of Elkanah, and she was barren. Her husband's other wife had children and loved to make Hannah feel miserable about her barrenness. When Hannah and her husband went to Shiloh to make their sacrifice for the year, Hannah could no longer hide her desperate desire.

One day, Elkanah was there offering a sacrifice, when Hannah began crying and refused to eat. So Elkanah asked, "Hannah, why are you crying? Why won't you eat? Why do you feel so bad? Don't I mean more to you than ten sons?" When the sacrifice had been offered, and they had eaten the meal, Hannah got up and went to pray. Eli was sitting in his chair near the door to the place of worship. Hannah was brokenhearted and was crying as she prayed, "LORD All-Powerful, I am your servant, but I am so miserable! Please let me have a son. I will give him to you for as long as he lives, and his hair will never be cut." Hannah prayed silently to the LORD for a long time. But her lips were moving, and Eli thought she was drunk. "How long are you going to stay drunk?" he asked. "Sober up!" "Sir, please don't think I'm no good!" Hannah answered. "I'm not drunk, and I haven't been drinking. But I do feel miserable and terribly upset. I've been praying all this time, telling the LORD about my problems." Eli replied, "You may go home now and stop worrying. I'm sure the God of Israel will answer your prayer." "Sir, thank you for being so kind to me,"

Hannah said. Then she left, and after eating something, she felt much better (1 Sam. 1:7-18).

We get what we need when our requests can fulfill God's need as well. Hannah had a need for fulfillment. She was so desperate for a change in her circumstances that she could not eat until she knew that God had heard her request. Her desperation also made her a target for misunderstanding. Eli thought her method of prayer must have come from someone who had lost control. He assumed she had been drinking, which of course was not the case.

Not only did Hannah have a need for a son, but at the same time God needed another Levite through whom He could bring back His voice to His people.

Later the LORD blessed Elkanah and Hannah with a son. She named him Samuel because she had asked the LORD for him (vv. 19-20).

God rewards dedication by blessing with abundance those who keep their word, as we see in the next verses.

When it was the time of the year to go to Shiloh again, Hannah and Elkanah took Samuel to the LORD's house. They brought along a three-year-old bull, a twenty-pound sack of flour, and a clay jar full of wine. Hannah and Elkanah offered the bull as a sacrifice, then brought the little boy to Eli. "Sir," Hannah said, "a few years ago I stood here beside you and asked the LORD to give me a child. Here he is! The LORD gave me just what I asked for. Now I am giving him to the LORD, and he will be the LORD's servant for as long as he lives." The

LORD was kind to Hannah, and she had three more sons and two daughters. But Samuel grew up at the LORD's house in Shiloh (vv. 24-28; 2:21).

Hannah showed how her dedication to God continued through ongoing investment in Samuel's life. Each year she visited him and took him a special linen garment that she had made. Hannah focused on her gratitude for the answered prayer. Samuel, as well, paid a price for his mother's decision. As a result of having been set apart, or dedicated, as a child, Samuel suffered a series of separations from those he loved.

*Samuel was separated from his family.* He was the one given to the work of God, serving in the Temple. And although he had no choice in the matter of being dedicated, his position made him privy to a relationship with God. As he grew older, his dedication was evident in his willingness to serve faithfully.

Samuel served the LORD by helping Eli the priest, who was by that time almost blind. In those days, the LORD hardly ever spoke directly to people, and he did not appear to them in dreams very often. But one night, Eli was asleep in his room, and Samuel was sleeping on a mat near the sacred chest in the LORD's house. They had not been asleep very long when the LORD called out Samuel's name. "Here I am!" Samuel answered (3:1-4).

*Samuel was separated from his leader.* After God tested Samuel's hearing, He tested Samuel's loyalty. Samuel's honesty in communicating the word of God to Eli was meant to reveal whether Samuel's natural relationships would hinder his ability to serve the Lord with complete, unhindered dedication.

The LORD then stood beside Samuel and called out as he had done before, "Samuel! Samuel!" "I'm listening," Samuel answered. "What do you want me to do?" (v. 10).

In verses 11-14, God told Samuel of the judgment that would come upon Eli the high priest and his family. Little Samuel was afraid to tell Eli what God had told him, but he was truthful when Eli asked. Eli was like a father to Samuel, so this test must have been very difficult to navigate for this young boy who had no other close attachments. But Samuel proved his dedication through his loyalty to the sovereignty of God. Samuel followed God's instruction exactly, even when it meant possibly isolating himself further from Eli.

As Samuel grew up, the LORD helped him and made everything Samuel said come true. From the town of Dan in the north to the town of Beersheba in the south, everyone in the country knew that Samuel was truly the LORD's prophet. The LORD often appeared to Samuel at Shiloh and told him what to say. Then Samuel would speak to the whole nation of Israel (3:19—4:1).

## Missing the Mantle

*Samuel was separated from his sons.* Samuel was most vulnerable and missed the mantle when it came to his children. Although he had dedicated his own life to the work of the priesthood, his sons did not walk in his ways.

Samuel had two sons. The older one was Joel, and the younger one was Abijah. When Samuel was getting old, he let them be leaders at Beersheba. But they were not like their father. They were dishonest and accepted bribes to give unfair decisions. One day the nation's leaders came to Samuel at Ramah and said, "You are an old man. You set a good example for your sons, but they haven't followed it. Now we want a king to be our leader, just like all the other nations. Choose one for us!" (8:1-5).

We can demonstrate dedication by our lifestyle, but we cannot force it on others or pass it on. And even though we can dedicate our children to the Lord when they are young, that is only the beginning. They have to choose the quality of dedication for themselves.

## Modeling the Mantle

When we carry the Word of God within us through understanding and experience, we model the power of dedication. With Samuel's history of dedication to God, there was no better choice when God called on him to anoint and set apart a shepherd for kingship. Through Samuel's dedication and intimate relationship with God, Samuel was empowered to anoint the first two kings of Israel: Saul and David.

Samuel took a small jar of olive oil and poured it on Saul's head. Then he kissed Saul and told him: "The LORD has chosen you to be the leader and ruler of his people" (10:1).

Samuel made an emotional connection with Saul. Later, when God rejected Saul as king, Samuel experienced the pain of separation once again. As the voice of the Lord to the children of

Israel, Samuel would need to replace Saul with God's choice.

> The LORD was sorry that he had made Saul the king of Israel. One day he said, "Samuel, I've rejected Saul, and I refuse to let him be king any longer. Stop feeling sad about him. Put some olive oil in a small container and go visit a man named Jesse, who lives in Bethlehem. I've chosen one of his sons to be my king." Jesse sent for David. He was a healthy, good-looking boy with a sparkle in his eyes. As soon as David came, the LORD told Samuel, "He's the one! Get up and pour the olive oil on his head." Samuel poured the oil on David's head while his brothers watched. At that moment, the Spirit of the LORD took control of David and stayed with him from then on (15:35–16:1; 16:12-13).

Finally, Samuel found a worthy man (David) who carried the same heart of dedication. What we must realize is that Samuel had a tough job as leader of Israel. We see that he failed to find dedication when he looked for it in his family, and he failed to find it by looking on the outward appearance (Saul). In the end, only God could determine who was dedicated enough to become king of Israel.

## Questions to Consider

- ✎ Have you ever experienced separation from those whom you love because God was leading you toward His will?
- ✎ How would you measure your level of dedication to the will of God?
- ✎ Do some areas of your life suffer because of your

devotion and dedication to God?

 &#9702; Have you ever assumed someone's level of dedication based on the outward signs? What did you learn from that experience?

 &#9702; In what ways can you become more dedicated to the purposes of God in your life?

## Authority at a Glance

Wearing the mantle of dedication means that

 &#9702; you are set apart for a special purpose;

 &#9702; you will find your greatest satisfaction in putting God first;

 &#9702; you can become a target for misunderstanding;

 &#9702; you will raise the standard of devotion to God in the lives of others.

## Pattern for Prayer

Let's look at Psalm 16 as a pattern for prayer.

Protect me, LORD God! I run to you for safety, and I have said, "Only you are my Lord! Every good thing I have is a gift from you." Your people are wonderful, and they make me happy, but worshipers of other gods will have much sorrow. I refuse to offer sacrifices of blood to those gods or worship in their name. You, LORD, are all I want! You are my choice, and you keep me safe. You make my life pleasant, and my future is bright. I praise you, LORD, for being my guide. Even in the darkest night, your teachings fill my mind. I will always look to you, as you stand beside me and protect me from fear. With all my heart, I will celebrate, and I can safely rest. I am your chosen one. You won't leave me in the grave or let my body decay. You have shown me the path to life, and you make me glad by being near to me. Sitting at your right side, I will always be joyful.

# Declaration

- I will choose to take on God's view of my husband.
- I will see my husband wearing the mantle of Samuel.
- I will affirm my husband's calling to live a dedicated lifestyle.
- I will uphold my role by restoring my husband's authority.
- I will encourage my husband by building him up.

# Seal It with a Gift

In these ancient times that we've been studying, to be dedicated and anointed for a purpose meant that fragrant oil would be poured over your body, starting with the top of your head. As the oil ran from the head down upon the clothing, it marked the anointed one by setting him apart. My suggestion for this demonstration is to purchase a special fragrance for your husband, such as

- Cologne
- Room fragrance spray
- Scented massage oil

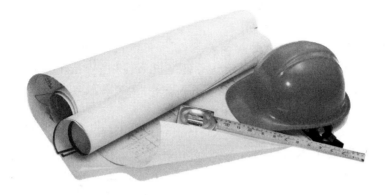

# CHAPTER 12

# DAVID: THE MANTLE OF WORSHIP

*And the Lord shall be King over all the earth. In that day there shall be one Lord—his name alone will be worshiped.*
ZECHARIAH 14:9, *TLB*

God doesn't require us to have a good singing voice, write beautiful poetry or be a graceful dancer. What real worship does require is that we focus everything we are on everything God is. That is the heart of worship. David's life teaches us that worship must be authentic and transparent. No matter what our sin, if we will run to God, then worship will become a refuge that lifts us from the depths of despair.

# Making the Mantle

David's life was defined by several roles: shepherd, warrior, musician, worshiper, king. Although God elevated him many times, authentic worship stayed with David throughout his life. Let's go back to where his story begins.

Familiarity with worship began for David in the fields of his father's land. There he was responsible to protect, defend and lead his father's sheep. It was not the highest and most honored position in the family; rather, it was assigned to David because he was the youngest. The sheep were not only farm animals to look after but also a representation of Israel's worship, since sheep were sacrificed in burnt offerings. David's acts of protection against the bear and the lion were spiritual as well as physical tests. In fact, David used his history with the sheep to convince King Saul of his ability to defeat Goliath.

> But David told him: "Your Majesty, I take care of my father's sheep. And when one of them is dragged off by a lion or a bear, I go after it and beat the wild animal until it lets the sheep go. If the wild animal turns and attacks me, I grab it by the throat and kill it. Sir, I have killed lions and bears that way, and I can kill this worthless Philistine. He shouldn't have made fun of the army of the living God! The LORD has rescued me from the claws of lions and bears, and he will keep me safe from the hands of this Philistine" (1 Sam. 17:34-37).

David's time of preparation and peace came in the fields, tending the sheep. This was his private time of worship. David's history as a worshiper prepared him for battle against a giant and provides us with a warning of a more devious enemy. The foe we should guard against comes to us before the battle by testing our boundaries of preparation and peace. David didn't go looking for trouble with wild animals—they came to him. He was guarding something very precious that they wanted to destroy. We need to remember that our first victories will not be on a battlefield but in the quiet fields, where we protect our times of private worship. If our worship is not defended daily, then it will be ravaged by life's consuming responsibilities. The boundaries of defense that David set around his sheep brought peace for the present and preparation for the future and were proof that he could protect and defend his worship.

When David volunteered to represent the Israelites by fighting Goliath, King Saul offered his armor. David showed great wisdom in choosing the tools of defense he had already proven effective. He could have fallen victim to fear because of the enormity of the enemy, but he rejected foreign systems of defense and chose to rely on the name of the Lord as he engaged in battle with a giant. David's declaration shows us that he knew the spiritual significance of this conflict and that he wasn't there to look powerful—he was there to defend God's sheep.

> David answered [Goliath]: "You've come out to fight me with a sword and a spear and a dagger. But I've come to fight you in the name of the LORD All-Powerful. He is the God of Israel's army, and you have insulted him too! Today the LORD will help me defeat you. I'll knock you down and cut off your head, and I'll feed the bodies of the other Philistine soldiers to the birds and wild animals. Then the whole world will know that Israel had a real God. Everybody here will see that the LORD doesn't need swords or spears to save his people. The LORD always wins his battles, and he will help us defeat you" (vv. 45-47).

David's years of solitude with the sheep formed a deep well of worship from which he drew sustenance for the rest of his life. David didn't tailor his mantle of worship for an audience of human onlookers; he gave his best to the Lord when no one was looking. This prepared him to give his best when the nation was watching him as their king.

Private moments of worship prepare us for public victories. No story plays out this truth with such vivid detail as David's. He used his time in the fields to worship and also to sharpen his gifts (or talents). One of those talents was playing the harp. His harp playing was good enough to bring him a kingly commendation. When King Saul was distraught and tormented by evil spirits, David would drive them away by playing his harp. He was obviously much more than a musician; he was also a worship warrior. His authority in the Spirit, which had been sharpened in private, was wielded in public defense of a king. Because of his time out in the fields, David would go forward to win many battles in the Spirit before he won them in the flesh.

## Missing the Mantle

David's worship was so authentic that God drew him out of obscurity as a demonstration of His watchful eye upon His people. There were more high points in David's life than one can count. For one, at a very young age he became a war hero who had slain a giant. He went on to defeat many enemies of God's people until he became king. Even after that, he continued with much creativity to expand the kingdom and his own household. Not many things could have brought such a vivacious king low, especially a king who focused on gratitude through worship. So what caused King David to sin in such a vile way as when he schemed to have Bathsheba as his own?

What made David such a dynamic worshiper was his ability to abandon all and lose himself in his appreciation for God and his desire for more of Him. Unfortunately, David's strength when used for God became his downfall when focused on someone else. David learned the hard way that worship is only holy and authentic when directed at a worthy God. Sadly, David lost his focus and began to "worship" a woman named Bathsheba.

> Late one afternoon, David got up from a nap and was walking around on the roof of his palace. A beautiful young woman was down below in her courtyard, bathing as her religion required. David happened to see her, and he sent one of his servants to find out who she was (2 Sam. 11:2-3).

David was not deterred from pursuing Bathsheba by the information he received about her marriage to Uriah the Hittite. Blatantly ignoring God's commandment against adultery, David sent for the woman and slept with her; then he returned her to her house. Not only did he commit adultery, but he also began to plot the cover-up when faced with a public declaration of his sin when he and Bathsheba had conceived a child while her husband was away at war.

By asking Bathsheba's husband, Uriah, to return home from the fighting to be with his wife, David believed that all would be forgotten, since Uriah (and others) would assume the baby was Uriah's. But David's plan fell apart when Uriah refused to sleep with his wife while his comrades were still on the battlefield fighting and dying. Instead, he slept outside the king's palace with the guards. After several failed attempts to manipulate Uriah to sleep with Bathsheba, David sent

Uriah back to the battlefield with a letter that was Uriah's own death warrant.

> The letter said: "Put Uriah on the front line where the fighting is the worst. Then pull the troops back from him, so that he will be wounded and die" (v. 15).

David's second ungodly desire in relation to Bathsheba came true when Uriah was killed in battle. David was guilty not only of turning his heart away from God but also of trying to cover his sin of adultery with murder. After David learned of Uriah's death and Bathsheba had mourned her husband, David brought her to the palace as his wife, and their son was soon born. For a short time all may have seemed forgotten, but God was angry with David for what he had done, so He sent Nathan the prophet to tell David a story.

Nathan described a poor man who had only one lamb. This man was taken advantage of by a rich man who had many lambs but who still desired the poor man's one and only lamb. In the end David was enraged at the rich man who had done such a thing.

> I swear by the living LORD that the man who did this deserves to die! And because he didn't have any pity on the poor man, he will have to pay four times what the lamb was worth (12:5-6).

In verse 7, Nathan the prophet responded to David by saying, "You are that rich man!" He went on to tell David everything God had witnessed against him with regard to Uriah and Bathsheba.

God turned David's deception upon him when He said,

"What you did was in secret, but I will do this in the open for everyone in Israel to see" (v. 12). David responded immediately with the words "I have disobeyed the Lord" (v. 13). David's instant honesty was a sign of authenticity; he was aware of himself and the vulnerability of his nature.

Nathan agreed: "Yes, you have! . . . You showed you didn't care what the Lord wanted. He has forgiven you, and you won't die. But your newborn son will" (vv. 13-14).

The prophecy transpired as Nathan said, and David and Bathsheba went on to have a second son—Solomon; but peace was never present in the house of David. Although we know that David was the most transparent, authentic worshiper in the Bible, it is clear that he was not free from the torment of sin and its consequences.

From the example of David's most vulnerable experience, we can learn that following your heart is only safe when your heart is focused on God. Our hearts cultivate our deepest desires. Although our hearts are fleshly portholes that God often uses to direct us, it is not spirit matter and thus can be corrupted and recreated. As we can see in the life of David, desires can easily rise within us and lead us astray. The knowledge of how deceitful a heart can be probably led David to pen one of the most memorable and effective prayers ever recorded for transformation of heart and spirit: "Create in me a pure heart, O God, and renew a steadfast spirit within me" (Ps. 51:10, *NIV*).

The most powerful lesson David can teach us is to be authentic when we approach God. Being real in worship—baring our hearts before Him—entreats God's blessing and brings His forgiveness. It is when we choose to be vulnerable before God through authenticity that He can answer our prayer for transformation. It is then that real worship is born in us and we reflect His nature.

It is so important to guard our hearts—not so much to protect the heart itself but to protect us from takeover by ungodly desire. God alone is worthy of our abandoned passion, even though we may find ourselves capable of letting go in other areas. The same attributes that made David worship with abandon were used for destruction when he turned his desire toward the beauty of a woman. That is when sin ensnared him and hid the truth of who he was. Only an enemy from within can turn authentic worship into a perversion and transparency into death and deception.

## Modeling the Mantle

David's greatest legacy was his desire to teach God's people how to worship God. When we read the psalms written by David, it is clear that his gratefulness is what moved him to worship the almighty God. He was absolutely jubilant in his praise when he moved the Ark of the Covenant to the capital city of Jerusalem.

> The people carrying the chest walked six steps, then David sacrificed an ox and a choice cow. He was dancing for the LORD with all his might, but he wore only a linen cloth. He and everyone else were celebrating by shouting and blowing horns while the chest was being carried along (2 Sam. 6:13-15).

David stretched people's comfort level regarding the form of his worship. His extravagant worship even brought criticism from his wife Michal. Yet when she expressed her disapproval for his actions, he responded by reaffirming his desire to honor

God: "The LORD chose me, and I was celebrating in honor of him" (v. 21).

David's desire was to make worship part of his people's everyday lives by building a temple to serve as a function of worship for God's people. Although David didn't actually get to build the tabernacle, he gathered the supplies and made the plans.

> David told the crowd: "God chose my son Solomon to build the temple, but Solomon is young and has no experience. This is not just any building—this is the temple for the LORD God! That's why I have done my best to get everything Solomon will need to build it—gold, silver, bronze, iron, wood, onyx, turquoise, colored gems, all kinds of precious stones, and marble" (1 Chron. 29:1-2).

David left everything to his son Solomon, who would have the pleasure of seeing his father's dream realized. As a form of worship, David gathered supplies, knowing that one day the people of God would gather and the Spirit of God would come dwell among David's people.

## Questions to Consider

- ✍ If worship is essentially spoken gratitude toward a sovereign God, then how do you worship if you are discontent?
- ✍ How do you worship when you are alone?
- ✍ If worship is an intimate investment, how intimate would you say you are?

    &#9043; How do you keep yourself authentic yet open to change?

## Authority at a Glance

Wearing the mantle of worship means that

- &#9043; you will live your most intimate moments with God away from the public eye;
- &#9043; you will approach God in an authentic way;
- &#9043; you will abandon inhibition in search of more of God;
- &#9043; you will worship your way through discontent;
- &#9043; you will understand the deceitfulness of the heart and may write or sing or pray in a way that shows great spiritual transformation.

## Pattern for Prayer

As we come to the close of this section, let's use Psalm 32 as our pattern for prayer.

> Our God, you bless everyone whose sins you forgive and wipe away. You bless them by saying, "You told me your sins, without trying to hide them, and now I forgive you." Before I confessed my sins, my bones felt limp, and I groaned all day long. Night and day your hand weighed heavily on me, and my strength was gone and in the summer heat. So I confessed my sins and told them all to you. I said, "I'll tell the LORD each one of my sins."

Then you forgave me and took away my guilt. We worship you, Lord, and we should always pray whenever we find out that we have sinned. Then we won't be swept away by a raging flood. You are my hiding place! You protect me from trouble, and you put songs in my heart because you have saved me. You said to me, "I will point out the road that you should follow. I will be your teacher and watch over you. Don't be stupid like horses and mules that must be led with ropes to make them obey." All kinds of troubles will strike the wicked, but your kindness shields those who trust you, LORD. And so your good people should celebrate and shout.

## Declarations

- I will choose to take on God's view of my husband.
- I will see my husband wearing the mantle of David.
- I will affirm my husband's calling to live a lifestyle of worship.
- I will uphold my role by restoring my husband's authority.
- I will encourage my husband by building him up.

## Seal It with a Gift

Here are gift suggestions for you and your husband to promote a spirit of worship and to create an authentic atmosphere in your home:

- A worship CD

- A treasure box in which to place a letter of encouragement to your husband (include praise—men love that!)

- Intimacy with your husband that is your idea! Spice things up a bit by telling him all the things you love about him. Tell him why you love his eyes or his hands, or tell the first memories you have of noticing the unique things about him. If this sounds uncomfortable, chances are this gift may take your relationship to a new level of intimacy and verbal communication.

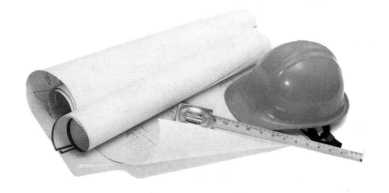

# CHAPTER 13

# SOLOMON: THE MANTLE OF WISDOM

*My mouth shall speak wisdom, and the meditation of my
heart shall give understanding.*
PSALM 49:3, *NKJV*

Like his father, David, Solomon was an extravagant worshiper.

Solomon loved the LORD and followed his father
David's instructions, but Solomon also offered sacrifices
and burned incense at the shrines. The most important
shrine was in Gibeon, and Solomon had offered more
than a thousand sacrifices on that altar. One night while
Solomon was in Gibeon, the LORD God appeared to him
in a dream and said, "Solomon, ask for anything you
want, and I will give it to you."

Solomon answered: "My father David, your servant, was honest and did what you commanded. You were always loyal to him, and you gave him a son who is now king. LORD God, I'm your servant, and you've made me king in my father's place. But I'm very young and know so little about being a leader. And now I must rule your chosen people, even though there are too many of them to count. Please make me wise and teach me the difference between right and wrong. Then I will know how to rule your people. If you don't, there is no way I could rule this great nation of yours."

God said: "Solomon, I'm pleased that you asked for this. You could have asked to live a long time or to be rich. Or you could have asked for your enemies to be destroyed. Instead, you asked for wisdom to make right decisions. So I'll make you wiser than anyone who has ever lived or ever will live. I'll also give you what you didn't ask for. You'll be rich and respected as long as you live, and you'll be greater than any other king. If you obey me and follow my commands, as your father David did, I'll let you live a long time" (1 Kings 3:3-14).

## Making the Mantle

Solomon's request showed humility and dependence upon God. Although he was young, Solomon was not arrogant in his own ability; he was fully aware of the need for great wisdom in order to make godly decisions.

Solomon was the son of King David and Bathsheba. Just as Solomon was conceived in a marriage begun with mistakes, so wisdom is often born out of our folly. Solomon prayed for wisdom to rule the kingdom his father had established. He knew that he needed wisdom to manage and expand the growth of a kingdom his father had sacrificed to gather for him.

Although worship was a legacy that Solomon received from his father and chose to continue, battle was not his style. Solomon chose to rule his kingdom with diplomacy, which would require treaties of peace with other nations.

> And the LORD gave Solomon wisdom, as he promised him: and there was peace between Hiram and Solomon; and they two made a league together (1 Kings 5:12, *KJV*).

Through these methods of diplomacy, Solomon thrived in wisdom as his kingdom expanded in abundance.

> There were so many people living in Judah and Israel while Solomon was king that they seemed like grains of sand on a beach. Everyone had enough to eat and drink, and they were happy. Solomon was brilliant. God had blessed him with insight and understanding. He was wiser than anyone else in the world, including the wisest people of the east and of Egypt. He was even wiser than Ethan the Ezrahite, and Mahol's three sons, Heman, Calcol, and Darda. Solomon became famous in every country around Judah and Israel. Solomon wrote three thousand wise sayings and composed more than one thousand songs. He could talk about all kinds of plants, from large trees to small bushes, and he taught about animals, birds, reptiles,

and fish. Kings all over the world heard about Solomon's wisdom and sent people to listen to him teach (4:20,29-34).

## Missing the Mantle

We know that David's vulnerability began when he followed his heart by honoring his own desire over the will of God. Like his father, David, Solomon's ultimate vulnerability came from trusting his ability to manage his affairs. His search for new solutions to diplomatic problems made him more susceptible to compromise. Most treaties that Solomon made with other kingdoms involved his receiving a wife as queen to seal the deal. Solomon's failure came about because he became elevated by his wisdom to a place where he no longer thought he needed to heed the instruction of the Lord.

> The LORD did not want the Israelites to worship foreign gods, so he had warned them not to marry anyone who was not from Israel. Solomon loved his wife, the daughter of the king of Egypt. But he also loved some women from Moab, Ammon, and Edom, and others from Sidon and the land of the Hittites. Seven hundred of his wives were daughters of kings, but he also married three hundred other women. As Solomon got older, some of his wives led him to worship their gods. He wasn't like his father David, who had worshiped only the LORD God. Solomon also worshiped Astarte the goddess of Sidon, and Milcom the disgusting god of Ammon. Solomon's father had obeyed the LORD with all his heart, but Solomon disobeyed and did

what the LORD hated. Solomon built shrines on a hill
east of Jerusalem. . . . In fact, he built a shrine for
each of his foreign wives, so all of them could burn
incense and offer sacrifices to their own gods (1 Kings
11:1-8).

Taking foreign wives backfired on Solomon when his desire
for peace included cohabitation with other gods. Instead of
Solomon's influencing his wives to worship in his way, his open-
mindedness led him to build for his wives places of pagan worship. God had specifically told Solomon not to take foreign
wives for this very reason.

The LORD God of Israel had appeared to Solomon two
times and warned him not to worship foreign gods. But
Solomon disobeyed and did it anyway. This made the
LORD very angry, and he said to Solomon: "You did what
you wanted and not what I told you to do. Now I'm
going to take your kingdom from you and give it to one
of your officials. But because David was your father, you
will remain king as long as you live" (11:9-12).

God is the source of all wisdom; wisdom loses its effective-
ness when we believe it releases us from simple obedience to
Him. Solomon lost sight of his commonsense priorities by
searching for something he already possessed. To go in search of
greater wisdom can overshadow what we already know to be
true. And because godly wisdom cannot cohabit with the foolishness of idolatry, Solomon's downfall came with the numer-
ous wives who opened his mind to false gods. Because Solomon
lacked spiritual boundaries in his personal life, God caused his
natural enemies to multiply. His kingdom was taken away as a

result of his being led away from God.

## Modeling the Mantle

Solomon may not have fought bloody battles with foreign enemies as his father had, but his struggles were just as real. Solomon's desire to use wisdom to avoid conflict led him to compromise himself, which was the greatest loss of all. Bloodshed would have been far better if it could have kept him from betraying his God.

The book of Proverbs is Solomon's journal of writings that describe his quest for more knowledge. In it he wrote:

> If you keep being stubborn after many warnings, you will suddenly discover you have gone too far. When justice rules a nation, everyone is glad; when injustice rules, everyone groans. If you love wisdom your parents will be glad, but chasing after bad women will cost you everything. An honest ruler makes the nation strong; a ruler who takes bribes will bring it to ruin (Prov. 29:1-4).

Not only did Solomon return to humility by charting his journey of vanity, but he also compared wisdom and folly in an effort to make sense of it all. These are Solomon's conclusions:

> I discovered that wisdom is better than foolishness, just as light is better than darkness. Wisdom is like having two good eyes; foolishness leaves you in the dark. But wise or foolish, we all end up the same. Finally, I said to myself, "Being wise got me nowhere! The same thing will

happen to me that happens to fools. Nothing makes sense. Wise or foolish, we all die and are soon forgotten." . . . It's just as senseless as chasing the wind (Eccles. 2:13-17).

As we follow Solomon's thought process, we see that he realized that all of his wealth that was accumulated through wisdom would be lost when he died. He questioned what all his work was for if he could not control who would receive what he had to pass along. Ecclesiastes 2:24-26 shows us that he came to a balanced conclusion, which reflected his knowledge that life was folly without God:

> The best thing we can do is to enjoy eating, drinking, and working. I believe these are God's gifts to us, and no one enjoys eating and living more than I do. If we please God, he will make us wise, understanding, and happy. But if we sin, God will make us struggle for a living, then he will give all we own to someone who pleases him. This makes no more sense than chasing the wind.

Although Solomon raised more questions than answers, we see that desiring to know the thoughts of God is as ineffective as chasing after the wind. It is ridiculous to believe that we can understand the ways of a holy, eternal, all-knowing God. When wisdom leads us to stupidity and foolishness, it has taken us away from God, who is the source of all true wisdom and knowledge.

> For wisdom is a defense as money is a defense, but the excellence of knowledge is that wisdom gives life to those that have it (Eccles. 7:12, *NKJV*).

## Questions to Consider

- How can wisdom add to your life?
- Does wisdom lead to wealth?
- What did Solomon mean by "chasing the wind"?
- What common attribute is often lost to those with great wisdom?

## Authority at a Glance

Wearing the mantle of wisdom means that

- you will seek answers before you raise questions;
- you will be able to find the balance between thoughtful action and abandoned, extravagant worship;
- your life will reflect control and peace;
- you will fail if you let pride replace God's instructions.

## Pattern for Prayer

- My heart is full of thanksgiving when I realize the power of the wisdom You have bestowed on us as women.
- I know that the quality of my life will hinge on my ability to receive Your wisdom.
- Father, along with the wisdom You give, add understanding that I may have the knowledge to apply it to my life.

# Declarations

- ☙ I will choose to take on God's view of my husband.
- ☙ I will see my husband wearing the mantle of Solomon.
- ☙ I will affirm my husband's calling to walk in wisdom.
- ☙ I will uphold my role by restoring my husband's authority.
- ☙ I will encourage my husband by building him up.

And the spirit of the LORD shall rest upon him, the spirit of wisdom and understanding, the spirit of counsel and might, the spirit of knowledge and of the fear of the LORD (Isa. 11:2, *KJV*).

# Seal It with a Gift

The greatest source of wisdom is the Word of God. For this mantle, I recommend that you buy your husband a new Bible. If he has recently purchased one, then you may want to buy a book that expands on the wisdom of the Bible.

- ☙ Personalized Bible
- ☙ Christian book
- ☙ Framed Scripture or plaque to hang on the wall or set on a stand

# Authenticity by Design

Make this challenge as simple or as elaborate as you like. The main thing to remember is that since we are a bridge from the past to the future, it is our duty and honor to equip our children with as much knowledge about their ancestry as possible. Historical pictures or objects in your home will bring a lot of attention from visitors, especially when you can give a little story or history to go along!

**Design goal:** To incorporate something historical or aged into every room in your home.

You can include history in the following ways:

1. Frame pictures of your ancestors or put their belongings on display.
2. Buy and restore antiques—furniture, china and other dishes, vintage jewelry, old books.
3. Collect prints or paintings of historical happenings.

The best places to look for old things are flea markets, trade-day markets, auctions and thrift stores. My brother has one of the coolest bachelor pads. He bought an old, beat-up door at our local trade-day market and hung the door, with metal brackets, about four inches from the wall. On the wall behind the door, he mounted a lighting device. The door has become a unique but functional work of art.

PART 5

*Design Element:*

# BALANCE

*Let me be weighed in an even balance, that God
may know mine integrity.*
JOB 31:6, *KJV*

*Without the private world of retreat, man becomes
virtually an unbalanced creature.*
ELEANOR MCMILLEN BROWN

When decorating in the Italian style, balance is its essence, as
this quote from Jane Gordon Clark so clearly emphasizes.

Italian rooms are beautifully proportioned; the height of
the ceiling, the size and layout of the architectural fea-
tures—the fireplace, windows, and the doors—have all

been carefully calculated to create a sense of harmony and balance. Similar care is taken when furnishing a room.

Furniture and pictures can be placed in such a way to emphasize the balance, with matching pairs arranged symmetrically, like mirror images. But equilibrium does not always dictate arrangements in pairs. Sometimes harmony is suggested by placing different but balanced objects in the room as if an old-fashioned scale was loaded with a number of small objects on one side and a single massive object on the other, but each of equal weight. Italians seem to do this as much by instinct as by design.[1]

**Note**

1. Jane Gordon Clark, *Italian Style* (Holbrook, MA: Adams Media Corporation, 1999), p. 31.

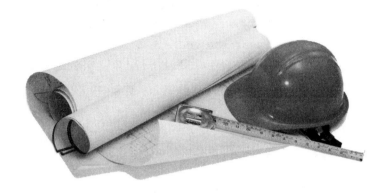

# CHAPTER 14

# ELIJAH: THE MANTLE OF CONFRONTATION

*The art of living is a priceless achievement worth all the courage it requires.*

ALEXANDRA STODDARD

Scripture introduces us to Elijah the prophet after King Ahab and his wife, Jezebel, began to set up their worship to Baal, a false god of the Canaanites.

> Ahab did more things to disobey the LORD than any king before him. He acted just like Jeroboam. Even worse, he married Jezebel the daughter of King Ethbaal

of Sidon and started worshiping Baal. Ahab built an altar and temple for Baal in Samaria and set up a sacred pole for worshiping the goddess Asherah. Ahab did more to make the LORD God of Israel angry than any other king of Israel before him (1 Kings 16:30-33).

# Making the Mantle

As a result of betrayal from the leadership of Israel, God raised up a prophet—Elijah—to confront compromise head-on.

> Elijah was a prophet from Tishbe in Gilead. One day he went to King Ahab and said, "I'm a servant of the living LORD, the God of Israel. And I swear in his name that it won't rain until I say so. There won't even be any dew on the ground" (17:1).

The spirit of Elijah was, in essence, strength represented by bearing a standard against the wickedness that threatened to displace God among His people. God honored Elijah and sent him to Sidon to keep him safe from King Ahab and Jezebel until God's word was fulfilled. During this time, God sent him to the home of a widow who was on her way to prepare her last meal.

> "Would you please bring me a cup of water?" [Elijah] asked. As she left to get it, he asked, "Would you also please bring me a piece of bread?" The widow answered, "In the name of the living LORD your God, I swear that I don't have any bread. All I have is a handful of flour and a little olive oil. I'm on my way home now with these few sticks to cook what I have for my son and me. After that,

we will starve to death" (17:10-12).

Elijah told her to return home and make herself and her son a cake, but not before making one for him. Scripture says, "The widow went home and did exactly what Elijah had told her. She and Elijah and her family had enough food for a long time" (v. 15).

Several days later, the women's son fell ill and died. Believing that it was judgment, she in turn blamed the prophet for her son's death. Elijah asked her to bring her son to him, and then he took the boy upstairs to pray for him. Verse 22 tells us the result: "The Lord answered Elijah's prayer, and the boy started breathing again."

As a prophet who spoke to kings and brought judgment on God's behalf, Elijah learned that even though what he spoke of happened, he was not the cause of the suffering of such judgment. He was only a messenger who brought with him the power of God and who could work miracles of intervention to bring prosperity and healing to those who would receive him. For King Ahab, who worked at making God—and His prophets—unwelcome, Elijah was an adversary.

For three years no rain fell in Samaria, and there was almost nothing to eat anywhere. The LORD said to Elijah, "Go and meet with King Ahab. I will soon make it rain." So Elijah went to see Ahab. Ahab went to meet Elijah, and when he saw him, Ahab shouted, "There you are, the biggest troublemaker in Israel!"

Elijah answered: "You're the troublemaker—not me! You and your family have disobeyed the LORD's commands by worshiping Baal. Call together everyone from Israel and have them meet me on Mount Carmel. Be sure to bring along the four hundred fifty prophets of Baal and the four hundred prophets of Asherah who eat at Jezebel's table."

Ahab got everyone together, then they went to meet Elijah on Mount Carmel. Elijah stood in front of them and said, "How much longer will you try to have things both ways? If the LORD is God, worship him! But if Baal is God, worship him!" (1 Kings 18:1-2,16-21).

Elijah arranged for the prophets of Baal, as well as for himself, to prepare sacrifices and place them upon the altars. Whoever prayed and received an answer of fire upon the sacrifice would be representing the true God. Elijah gave the false prophets all morning to pray before he began to chide them about their obviously impotent and nonexistent god.

> "Maybe he's daydreaming or using the toilet or traveling somewhere. Or maybe he's asleep, and you have to wake him up." The prophets kept shouting louder and louder, and they cut themselves with swords and knives until they were bleeding. This was the way they worshiped, and they kept it up all afternoon. But there was no answer of any kind (vv. 27-29).

Elijah told everyone to gather around him while he repaired the Lord's altar. He used 12 stones, representing the 12 tribes of Israel. He then carved a ditch around the altar of stones and poured water on the sacrifice until the water ran over and filled the ditch. Elijah prayed, and God sent fire to consume the sacrifice and dry up all the water surrounding it.

> When the crowd saw what had happened, they all bowed down and shouted, "The LORD is God! The LORD is God!" (v. 39).

# Missing the Mantle

Following his great victory, something in Elijah changed that caused him to seem as vulnerable as a lost child. After killing all the prophets of Baal, he ran away in fear of the wrath of Jezebel. He must have panicked when he heard the people shout their belief in God, for he knew that Jezebel was not going to be stopped by public opinion; she would be out for revenge, and Elijah would be her target. Indeed, Jezebel declared in 1 Kings 19:2, "You killed my prophets. Now I am going to kill you!"

The impact of her threat on Elijah might confuse us, because he had already faced many frightful events without backing down. So what caused him to run now? God wanted to know the same thing.

> "Elijah, why are you here?" [Elijah] answered, "LORD God All-Powerful, I've always done my best to obey you. But your people have broken their solemn promise to you. They have torn down your altars and killed all your prophets, except me. And now they are even trying to kill me!"
>
> The LORD said: "Elijah, you can go back to the desert near Damascus. And when you get there, appoint Hazael to be king of Syria. Then appoint Jehu son of Nimshi to be king of Israel, and Elisha son of Shaphat to take your place as my prophet. Hazael will start killing the people who worship Baal. Jehu will kill those who escape from Hazael, and Elisha will kill those who escape from Jehu. But seven thousand Israelites have refused to worship Baal, and they will live" (1 Kings 19:9-10,15-18).

What we can see from God's directive is that Elijah was

weary of fighting a battle alone. Being confrontational causes us to see only the negative, because the negative is what needs to be corrected. So Elijah felt lonely and isolated because of his stand against Jezebel and the god of Baal. God encouraged him by telling him to appoint these men who would take up the cause of killing the unrighteous.

God also pointed out the exact number of Israelites who had not compromised (7,000), and I am sure that information renewed Elijah's strength to fight, since he then knew he was not alone. Confronters are most vulnerable to giving up when they feel their efforts have separated them from their original cause. They can take great amounts of pressure and personal attack in order to obey the Lord until they begin to feel as though they are fighting for a lost cause. Discouragement comes rushing in when they are left to their own feelings of isolation and fear. God's sending Elijah to the widow's house in an earlier event was probably for his own mental stability as well as to bless her.

## Modeling the Mantle

Elijah's next test of confrontation may not have been the show-stopper everyone expected after he had stopped the rain and called down fire. This time, God asked him to face the king and his wife who had caused him to run away.

King Ahab and Jezebel had continued in their ways of injustice, but God did not want them to forget Him, so He sent Elijah to confront the situation.

The LORD said to Elijah the prophet, "King Ahab of Israel is in Naboth's vineyard right now, taking it over. Go tell him that I say, 'Ahab, you murdered Naboth and

took his property. And so, in the very spot where dogs licked up Naboth's blood, they will lick up your blood.'"
When Elijah found him, Ahab said, "So, my enemy, you found me at last."

Elijah answered: "Yes, I did! Ahab, you have managed to do everything the Lord hates. Now you will be punished."

When Ahab heard this, he tore his clothes and wore sackcloth day and night. He was depressed and refused to eat. Some time later, the LORD said, "Elijah, do you see how sorry Ahab is for what he did? I won't punish his family while he is still alive, I'll wait until his son is king" (1 Kings 21:17-21,27-29).

Elijah obeyed God and confronted his fear of facing Ahab and Jezebel. During Elijah's lowest moment of despair, God gave him instructions to appoint Hazael, Jehu and Elisha. Although we soon see the legacy that Elijah left to Elisha, we must remember that later Hazael killed Benhadad and Jehu killed Jezebel and all of Ahab's descendants (see 2 Kings 8:7-15; 9:30—10:17). Although the victory over evil came after Elijah was taken away, his enemy's appointment with death came by Elijah's overcoming his own fears and by his appointing the three men as his companions of confrontation.

## Questions to Consider

ᴈ Do you avoid confrontation?

ᴈ What have you learned from the account of Elijah about godly confrontation?

- Have you ever felt you were alone after you made a righteous judgment?
- Has reminding others of their purpose ever made you feel like public enemy number one?

## Authority at a Glance

Wearing the mantle of confrontation means that

- you will be a standard-bearer against wickedness;
- you will be called to reveal what needs to be corrected;
- you will be most vulnerable when your efforts separate you from your cause;
- you must face your fear of man head-on.

## Pattern for Prayer

- Father, I thank You for giving me insight into confrontation.
- Show me how to build my confrontation skills, and keep me from destruction that comes through denial.
- I acknowledge the fruit of confrontation in the life of Elijah, and I ask to receive a double portion of his anointing.
- I willingly walk in submission to Your will.
- Let my life demonstrate Your power of transformation and impartation as I endeavor to encourage my husband's ability to confront.

# Elijah's Prayer of Confrontation

Our LORD, you are the God of Abraham, Isaac, and Israel. Now, prove that you are the God of this nation, and that I, your servant, have done this at your command. Please answer me, so these people will know that you are the LORD God, and that you will turn their hearts back to you (1 Kings 18:36-37).

# Declarations

- I will choose to take on God's view of my husband.
- I will see my husband wearing the mantle of Elijah.
- I will affirm my husband's calling to walk by faith.
- I will uphold my role by restoring my husband's authority.
- I will encourage my husband by building him up.

# Seal It with a Gift

Elijah was a man of the elements. Think of water, rain, fire and wind as you choose a gift for your husband. I recommend that you buy him a gift that incorporates one of the four elements.

- Umbrella
- Chiminea (an outdoor fireplace)
- Bedside fountain (the relaxing water sounds encourage rest)

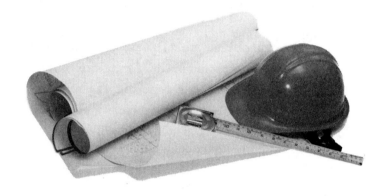

# CHAPTER 15

# DANIEL: THE MANTLE OF INTERPRETATION

*The possibility of interpretation lies in the identity of the observer with the observed. Each material thing has its celestial side; has its translation, through humanity, into the spiritual and necessary sphere, where it plays a part as indestructible as any other.*
RALPH WALDO EMERSON

Daniel is probably best remembered as the man who stayed one night in a den of lions and who lived to talk about it. But the Bible portrays Daniel as a very layered and complex character whose life as a young man had been spent as a captive of the Babylonians.

In the third year that Jehoiakim was king of Judah, King Nebuchadnezzar of Babylonia attacked Jerusalem. The Lord let Nebuchadnezzar capture Jehoiakim and take away some of the things used in God's temple. And when the king returned to Babylonia, he put these things in the temple of his own god. One day the king ordered Ashpenaz, his highest palace official, to choose some young men from the royal family of Judah and from other leading Jewish families. The king said, "They must be healthy, handsome, smart, wise, educated, and fit to serve in the royal palace. Teach them how to speak and write our language and give them the same food and wine that I am served. Train them for three years, and then they can become court officials." Four of the young Jews chosen were Daniel, Hananiah, Mishael, and Azaiah, all from the tribe of Judah. But the king's chief official gave them Babylonian names: Daniel became Belteshazzar, Hananiah became Shadrach, Mishael became Meshack, and Azaiah became Abednego (Dan. 1:1-7).

## Making the Mantle

God positioned His servants directly under the king to be his advisors. They were being prepared through diet and training to be healthy and ready to serve the king. It was their responsibility to continue their Jewish heritage while learning the ways of their foreign ruler. This balance was pivotal to their becoming quality interpreters. Daniel and his friends could not lose touch with the roots of their faith, so each decision that led them deeper into the culture of Babylonia had to be weighed against their history and their obedience to God. For Daniel, the first test was to find a way to eat according to his heritage without rebelling against the king's orders.

> Daniel made up his mind to eat and drink only what God had approved for his people to eat. And he asked the king's chief official for permission not to eat the food and wine served in the royal palace. God had made the official friendly and kind to Daniel. But the man still told him, "The king has decided what you must eat and drink. And I am afraid he will kill me, if you eat something else and end up looking worse than the other young men" (vv. 8-10).

Daniel found a way to negotiate with the guard who had been put in charge of his care.

> So Daniel said to the guard, "For the next ten days, let us have only vegetables and water at mealtime. When the ten days are up, compare how we look with the other young men, and decide what to do with us." The guard agreed to do what Daniel had asked. Ten days later, Daniel and his friends looked healthier and better than the young men who had been served food from the royal palace (vv. 11-15).

Daniel had found a way to obey the commandment of the Lord and to keep relationship with his authority. As a result, God made Daniel and the other three young men very wise.

At the end of the training period, King Nebuchadnezzar interviewed the four young men and found them to be far more impressive than the others in the program at the palace. He gave them the royal positions for which they had been groomed, and they served him whenever he needed advice.

Daniel's next level of leadership in interpretation was the deciphering of dreams and visions. In the second year of his reign, King Nebuchadnezzar became greatly disturbed by a nightmare. He did not understand the dream, so he called all of his advisors, magicians and counselors to give him the interpretation. The only catch was that he would not tell them the dream itself. He knew that the only way to receive the proper interpretation was to demand that the interpreter also know the dream without being told.

> "Your Majesty," [the magicians and advisors] said, "if you will only tell us your dream, we will interpret it for you." The king replied, "You're just stalling for time, because you know what's going to happen if you don't come up with the answer. You've decided to make up a bunch of lies, hoping I might change my mind. Now tell me the dream, and that will prove that you can interpret it." His advisors explained, "Your Majesty, you are demanding the impossible!" This made the king so angry that he gave orders for every wise man in Babylonia to be put to death, including Daniel and his three friends (2:7-10,12-13).

When Daniel was told that he and all of the advisors were about to be killed, he went to the king's official to ask for time to pray. After he left the official's presence, he went to his three friends to ask them to pray along with him for the mystery of the dream to be revealed so that all of the king's advisors would be spared.

God answered their prayers for mercy and showed Daniel in a vision what the king had been dreaming. Daniel rushed to the king's official to stop the execution of the advisors and to beg for an audience with the king. Arioch (the official) then took Daniel before the king and announced that he had found a man who could comply with the king's wishes.

> The king asked Daniel, "Can you tell me my dream and what it means?"
>
> Daniel answered: "Your Majesty, not even the smartest person in all the world can do what you are demanding. But the God who rules from heaven can explain mysteries. And while you were sleeping, he showed you what will happen in the future. However, you must realize that these mysteries weren't explained to me because I am smarter than everyone else. Instead, it was done so that you would understand what you have seen" (vv. 26-30).

Daniel went on to describe the ominous statue that King Nebuchadnezzar had seen in his dream, as well as the meaning behind every element of its figure. It was a prophetic picture of the kingdoms to come. The result of Daniel's ability to interpret prophecy through prayer brought him promotion from the king.

> The king said, "Now I know that your God is above all other gods and kings, because he gave you the power to explain this mystery." The king then presented Daniel with a lot of gifts; he promoted him to governor of Babylon Province and put him in charge of the other wise men. At Daniel's request, the king appointed Shadrach, Meshach, and Abednego to high positions in Babylon Province, and he let Daniel stay on as a palace official (vv. 47-49).

Daniel served three different rulers of what was then the

Babylonian Empire without forgetting the One he truly served—the God above all gods. Daniel showed accuracy in interpretation, and the king knew he could trust Daniel.

## Missing the Mantle

The natural vulnerability for interpreters is to mingle their personal feelings with God's message. We know that in Daniel's case he came to love the king as a friend and confidant, and maybe this is one reason for Nebuchadnezzar's negligence in heeding the warning from Daniel. Friendship can sometimes get in the way of what God is saying. If we speak sympathetically and haltingly, our relationship connection can add to our message a sense of mercy that God did not intend. When King Nebuchadnezzar had a dream about a tree that would be chopped down, Daniel interpreted it to refer to the king and his fall from sanity. He pleaded with the king to change his ways and thereby hold off the judgment of God: "Your Majesty, please be willing to do what I say. Turn from your sins and start living right; have mercy on those who are mistreated. Then all will go well with you for a long time" (4:27).

Despite Daniel's warning, the king declared his kingdom to have been built by his own power and for his own glory. As a result, God took from him the kingdom as well as his sanity. King Nebuchadnezzar lived as an animal for seven years before he acknowledged God as the most high and was healed and restored.

We cannot blame Daniel for the king's choices, but this analogy shines light on the vulnerability of being an interpreter. Although Daniel delivered a message of integrity to the king, the way in which it was delivered may have been compromised by the care of friendship. Sometimes perfect strangers can more accurately convey the conviction with which a message is borne from God. This may be why prophets are without honor in their own land. Due to their earthy attachments and reputations, they may be hindered in their calling to convey a message.

Daniel constantly wore the mantle of interpreter. Maybe he was less vulnerable than most because of his precarious situation of being in leadership while his countrymen were in exile. He saw both sides and used his spiritual heritage to speak only when God commanded. If only all of us feared death every time we spoke, then maybe our interpretation record would be as clean-cut as Daniel's!

## Modeling the Mantle

The gift of interpretation is the ability for one messenger to bridge separate streams of communication and accurately mesh them into one message. Daniel was this messenger, and sometimes his interpretations made him popular, while other times his accurate knowledge of a situation's meaning meant that he would risk his life to uphold God's word. Let's examine the ways in which Daniel upheld the law of the Lord, even in the face of death.

Many of us are familiar with the phrase "the handwriting is on the wall." Not everyone realizes, however, that the phrase originated in the book of Daniel. Belshazzar became king after his father, Nebuchadnezzar. On one particular occasion, he held a banquet. At this celebration, Belshazzar drank wine until he was drunk, and then he ordered his servants to bring the sacred silver and gold cups for his personal use. When the cups were brought in, those in attendance began to worship their idols. Immediately a hand began to write words on the wall, which stunned the king and made him feel faint. He then called all of his advisors and counselors to decipher the message on the wall. The king promised gifts and authority to the man who could translate the message, but no one could. As the king grew distraught, one of his wives comforted him with the reminder of Daniel and his ability to interpret. When Daniel was brought in to Belshazzar, he reminded him of his father's downfall, the need for repentance and the sin in knowing God while serving idols. Then Daniel read the writing on the wall and said:

> The words written there are *mene,* which means "numbered," *tekel,* which means "weighed," and *parsin,* which means "divided." God has numbered the days of your kingdom and has brought it to an end. He has weighed you on his balance scales, and you fall short of what it takes to be king. So God has divided your kingdom between the Medes and the Persians (5:25-28).

Just as Daniel had spoken, that very night the king was killed and a new king from Media became the ruler. His name was Darius. When Darius began setting up the system of government, he divided the kingdom into 120 states. He then appointed governors over each state, with three officials to oversee the governors. Daniel was one of the three officials set over the governors of the kingdom, and he did his job so efficiently that the king let Daniel govern the entire kingdom. This made all the other leaders angry and jealous of Daniel. As a result, Scripture tells us, "Finally, they said to one another, 'We will never be able to bring any charge against Daniel unless it has to do with his religion'" (6:5).

So they plotted against him by having the king pass a law forbidding the worship of any gods apart from the king for a

30-day period. The law was signed and sealed and could not be overturned. Daniel heard about the law, but it didn't stop him from praying when he returned home. He continued to pray at his window three times a day. When the jealous officials saw him, they told the king that Daniel the Jew was disobedient and would have to suffer the consequences.

Daniel was thrown into the den of lions. God could have stopped the conspiracy, but He didn't.

> At daybreak the king got up and ran to the pit. He was anxious and shouted, "Daniel, you were faithful and served your God. Was he able to save you from the lions?" (vv. 19-20).

The king was greatly relieved to see that, by a miracle from God, Daniel was indeed alive.

> King Darius then sent this message to all people of every nation and race in the world: "Greetings to all of you! I command everyone in my kingdom to worship and honor the God of Daniel. He is the living God, the one who lives forever. His power and his kingdom will never end. He rescues people and sets them free by working great miracles. Daniel's God has rescued him from the power of the lions" (vv. 25-27).

What an amazing letter from the king, which God inspired not through a dream this time but through Daniel's life! Daniel truly interpreted a real and living God who loves, cares for and protects His faithful followers. As Daniel's experiences show us, we don't always interpret someone else's message; sometimes we actually *become* the message.

# Questions to Consider

- ⊗ Have you ever had to balance yourself between two opinions?
- ⊗ Has your integrity ever made you feel as if you had been thrown into a den of lions?
- ⊗ Has God ever shown up for you in a mighty way or in the nick of time?

# Authority at a Glance

Wearing the mantle of interpretation means that

- ⊗ you will be able to obey the commandments of the Lord while keeping intact your relationship with those in authority over you;
- ⊗ you will recognize the power of corporate prayer;
- ⊗ you are emotionally vulnerable when your personal feelings get mingled with God's message.

# Pattern of Prayer

Take a look at Daniel's praise for the gift of interpretation, found in Daniel 2:20-23.

Our God, your name will be praised forever and forever. You are all-powerful, and you know everything. You control human events—you give rulers their power and take it away, and you are the source of wisdom and knowledge. You explain deep mysteries, because even the dark

is light to you. You are the God who was worshiped by
my ancestors. Now I thank you and praise you for making me wise and telling me the king's dream, together
with its meaning.

- ✍ God, I desire to be a messenger to speak for You.
- ✍ Give me courage to interpret Your will, both when it
  is popular and when it is not.
- ✍ I willingly hold up my vessel for You to fill that I may
  be poured out on Your people for Your glory.
- ✍ Let my life demonstrate Your power of transformation and impartation as I endeavor to encourage my
  husband's gift of interpretation.

## Declarations

- ✍ I will choose to take on God's view of my husband.
- ✍ I will see my husband wearing the mantle of Daniel.
- ✍ I will affirm my husband's calling to see all sides of an
  issue.
- ✍ I will uphold my role by restoring my husband's
  authority.
- ✍ I will encourage my husband by building him up.

## Seal It with a Gift

It is important, when given the gift of interpretation, that we
also have in our possession the tools to decipher and learn. Get
a book on personalities for you and your husband to read
together. He will become interested when you are excited about

all you have learned about him and his uniqueness. I have a favorite book when it comes to this topic. In my opinion, it is the best, most thorough manual on personality profiles:

    🙟 Fred and Anna Kendall, *Speaking of Love* (Nashville, TN: Thomas Nelson Publishers, 1995).

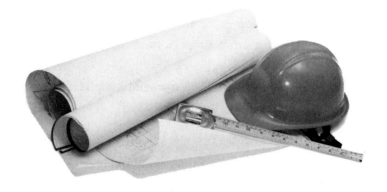

# NEHEMIAH: THE MANTLE OF LEADERSHIP

*A leader of good judgment gives stability; an exploiting
leader leaves a trail of waste.*
PROVERBS 29:4, *THE MESSAGE*

In both leadership and interior design, you must be able to confront the issues, interpret the answers and lead the way to change. Whether you are attempting a home renovation or a relationship restoration, leadership is an essential quality to possess. Let's see what leadership lessons can be learned from the servant Nehemiah.

# Making the Mantle

Nehemiah was a trusted cupbearer of King Artaxerxes. This job was performed for the protection of the king and was an important and well-respected position. But when Nehemiah heard the news from his brother that Jerusalem's walls lay in ruins, he became very troubled and prayed that God would give him favor with the king so that he could return to Jerusalem and lead the restoration of the walls.

One day, when Nehemiah was serving the king his wine, the king noticed that Nehemiah was acting unusual. He asked why Nehemiah looked so sad and then learned about the trouble in Nehemiah's homeland. The king inquired what could be done, and Nehemiah asked permission to go home. After finding out the timeline of Nehemiah's journey and the supplies he would require, the king sent him out with letters of permission. Nehemiah left with the blessing of his leader.

> The king sent some army officers and cavalry troops along with me, and as I traveled through the Western Provinces, I gave the letters to the governors. But when Sanballat from Horon and Tobiah the Ammonite official heard about what had happened, they became very angry, because they didn't want anyone to help the people of Israel. Three days after arriving in Jerusalem, I got up during the night and left my house. I took some men with me, without telling anyone what I thought God wanted me to do for the city (Neh. 2:9-12).

As we read Nehemiah's observations, we see that he was careful to observe the situation from every possible angle.

I went through Valley Gate on the west, then south past Dragon Spring, before coming to Garbage Gate. As I rode along, I took a good look at the crumbled walls of the city and the gates that had been torn down and burned. On the east side of the city, I headed north to Fountain Gate and King's Pool, but then the trail became too narrow for my donkey (vv. 13-14).

Nehemiah was careful to gather all the facts before he spoke to anyone about the situation.

None of the city officials knew what I had in mind. And I had not even told any of the Jews—not the priests, the leaders, the officials, or any other Jews who would be helping in the work. But when I got back, I said to them, "Jerusalem is truly in a mess! The gates have been torn down and burned, and everything is in ruins. We must rebuild the city wall so that we can again take pride in our city." Then I told them how kind God had been and what the king had said. Immediately, they replied, "Let's start building now!" So they got everything ready (vv. 16-18).

Throughout the rebuilding of the city's walls, Nehemiah encouraged teamwork. Nehemiah 3 tells about all who converged on a chosen section and took ownership of the restoration, including Levites, priests, families, rulers, goldsmiths and perfume makers.

Nehemiah kept track of the assigned volunteers and their particular section of the wall. What an undertaking it must have been just to plan the restoration and then gather the manpower to do it!

When the opposition to doing God's work came—as it always does—Nehemiah was ready with an answer.

When Sanballat, Tobiah, and Geshem the Arab heard
about our plans, they started insulting us and saying,
"Just look at you! Do you plan to rebuild the walls
of the city and rebel against the king?" I answered,
"We are servants of the God who rules from heaven,
and he will make our work succeed. So we will start
rebuilding Jerusalem, but you have no right to any of
its property, because you have had no part in its history" (vv. 19-20).

When change is introduced through leadership, enemies of
progress will emerge. Leadership is never easy, and this project
was no exception. Nehemiah's leadership produced enemies.

When Sanballat, the governor of Samaria, heard that we
were rebuilding the walls of Jerusalem, he became angry
and started insulting our people. But Sanballat, Tobiah,
the Arabs, the Ammonites, and the people from the city
of Ashdod saw the walls going up and the holes being
repaired. So they became angry and decided to stir up
trouble, and to fight against the people of Jerusalem.
But we kept on praying to our God, and we also sta-
tioned guards day and night (4:1,7-9).

## Missing the Mantle

The essence of leadership is the ability to use our strengths to
make a difference. While doing so, leaders can become vulnerable when they lack awareness of their deficits or weaknesses.
Let's take a look at how Nehemiah faced his areas of vulnerability and went to work to build them up.

On at least ten different occasions, the Jews living near
our enemies warned us against attacks from every side,
and so I sent people to guard the wall at its lowest places
and where there were still holes in it. I placed them
according to families, and they stood guard with swords
and spears and with bows and arrows. From then on, I
let half of the young men work while the other half
stood guard. They wore armor. Even the workers who
were rebuilding the wall strapped on a sword (vv. 12-
13,16,18).

Being a leader also requires a plan of defense regarding the
work to which God has called us, as we can clearly see in
Nehemiah's case.

## Modeling the Mantle

Regardless of opposition and ongoing challenges to the rebuilding efforts, Nehemiah finished strong.

On the twenty-fifth day of the month Elul, the wall was
completely rebuilt. It had taken fifty-two days. When
our enemies in the surrounding nations learned that the
work was finished, they felt helpless, because they knew
that our God had helped us rebuild the wall (6:15-16).

And so, with the work at last completed, the prophet
Nehemiah gathered the people together to continue the restoration process.

Although Jerusalem covered a large area, not many people lived there, and no new houses had been built. So God gave me the idea to bring together the people, their leaders, and officials and to check the family records of those who had returned from captivity in Babylonia, after having been taken there by King Nebuchadnezzar. There were 42,360 who returned, in addition to 7,337 servants, and 245 musicians. And so, by the seventh month, priests, Levites, temple guards, musicians, workers, and many of the ordinary people had settled in the towns of Judah (7:4-6,66,73).

After many years of exile, the children of Israel finally had a home of their own. They found they could live in peace once again because of the wall of protection that Nehemiah's leadership had provided them.

## Questions to Consider

- How did Nehemiah encourage teamwork?
- Have you ever left a leader without his or her blessing?
- Has your leadership ever created enemies?
- Have you ever had a cause worth taking a demotion to uphold?

## Authority at a Glance

Wearing the mantle of leadership means that

- you are not above answering to authority;

- you will quietly observe and look at every angle;
- you will get all the facts before you speak;
- you will have an answer ready for your opposition;
- you will defend your investment;
- you will gather people together;
- you will finish strong.

## Pattern for Prayer

- Father, I desire to be a woman of influence.
- I want to lead while being led by You.
- Help me lead myself so that I can lead others.
- I will not back up or cower under pressure.
- I need Your empowerment.

## Declarations

- I will choose to take on God's view of my husband.
- I will see my husband wearing the mantle of Nehemiah.
- I will affirm my husband's calling to lead by example.
- I will uphold my role by restoring my husband's authority.
- I will encourage my husband by building him up.

## Seal It with a Gift

A befitting gift for a man who is becoming a leader is a system of organization. Here are my gift recommendations:

- An organizer or calendar
- Strategy games and books
- A framed picture of a leadership motto for his desk or office

# Balance by Design

**Design goal:** To artfully arrange tabletops or bookshelves and wall art

Your optimum goal is to assemble a tablescape—a vignette on a tabletop—or wall art that pleases you each time you look at it. You may want to change the arrangement from time to time; but if you have the formula right, you can reassemble a beautiful vignette again and again. The best items to use are ones of various heights and shapes. I suggest three vertical items; for example:

- 1 tall vase or urn
- 1 pillar candle
- 1 bookend or small statue

Then gather 3 to 5 books and 3 to 5 framed pictures—1 small, 1 medium and 1 large. A small low arrangement would also be nice.

1.  Put your tallest item in the center of the table. Place a stack of three books next to the vase (spines out so that you can read the titles). The second tallest item is placed on the opposite side of the stack of books. Place the bookend or statue on top of the books. Lean the other two books against a sturdy tall item and place your medium framed picture in front to hold it in place.
2.  Angle your large framed picture at the corner of your first stack of books and your smallest picture in front of the pillar candle. Now step back and see

whether the grouping looks balanced. If not, everything may need to be pulled in closer to the center or pushed out a bit (based on the size and scale of your table). The last step is to check for angle. The vignette should be diagonally set, not parallel to the longest sides. (In other words, the edge of the stack of three books should be parallel to the corners of the table.) To achieve the best look, move the vignette by hugging it to keep it together and moving it to one side or the other.

3. When you step back to see how the whole room looks and how this tabletop arrangement balances with the room, you may discover that you need an additional texture. I would suggest adding a scarf or a small throw as a base under the elements on the table. Use a color from your curtains or couch pillows. Adding this texture will create softness and possibly balance the color in your room. To place it, clear the table and lay the scarf or throw on a diagonal; then add each item, scrunching up the fabric as you go. Leave one corner hanging off the edge of the table.

## End Tables

For end tables, use three books, one medium picture frame, one candle (any reasonable size) and a small decorative item. Assuming that there will be a lamp on the end table (you don't need one for this), place the books at an angle to the lamp base and place the candle on top. Place the picture frame to the side of the stack of books (angled), and then place the small decorative item in front of the picture frame.

## Hanging Single Pictures

The best tip for hanging single pictures is to be sure that the main image in a picture is eye level for a person of about 5' 7" to 6' tall. Center pictures on a blank wall or between the nearest edges. For example: If there is a window on the wall next to the space where the picture will be hung, you would center the picture between the window and the end of the wall.

## Hanging Groupings of Pictures

As a representation of the wall you are considering, draw a tic-tac-toe shape on a piece of paper, and then number the squares from top left to bottom right. You will end up with the top row as 1, 2, 3, the second row as 4, 5, 6 and the third row as 7, 8, 9.

A diamond-shaped pattern can be achieved by hanging pictures in squares 2, 4, 5, 6 and 8. Or you could hang pictures of different shapes, but make sure that the shapes are the same on the diagonal corners. For example, make 1 and 9 the same and 3 and 7 the same. If you do not want to fill each quadrant, then eliminate the pictures in the even squares. Example: Leave a blank space in squares 2, 4, 6 and 8. Note: The second row is your midline for height. For 8x10- to 11x17-inch pictures, hang them about 2 inches apart. Be consistent in spacing. For bigger pictures, hang them further apart; for smaller pictures, hang them closer together. Don't be afraid to hang different styles of frames together.

P A R T 6

*Design Element:*

# FUNCTION

*Have nothing in your houses which you do not know to be useful or believe to be beautiful.*
WILLIAM MORRIS

*What's practical is beautiful . . . and suitability always overrules fashion.*
BILLY BALDWIN

A well-known designer with more than 30 years of experience spoke to me about the importance of knowing the original use and function for a decorative piece of furniture when placing it in the home.

For example, within medieval castles there were not many ways to conceal items when they were not in use, so decorative pieces of furniture were large and designed to conceal specific items. Though most of us today use armoires to conceal televisions or linens or coats, their original use was much more defensive in nature. An armoire was originally designed to hold armor and was customarily placed in the bedroom. This was to ensure a nobleman's ready ability to defend the castle if it came under attack, without the possibility of being separated from his weapons of defense.

Today, the bedroom is also our last line of defense and the first place to begin our methods of protecting our marriages. As wives we must suit up for the cause and engage ourselves in the action. We must daily remember that our marriages are covenants established by God and hated by an ancient enemy who desires our downfall. Passion should be the first place we go when our marriage is besieged. Sexual intimacy doesn't fix every marital problem, but it is a good place to stoke the fire when the castle gets cold.

# CHAPTER 17

# JOHN THE BAPTIST: THE MANTLE OF PASSION

*Because you kept my Word in passionate patience, I'll keep you safe in the time of testing that will be here soon, and all over the earth, every man, woman, and child put to the test.*
REVELATION 3:10, *THE MESSAGE*

Passion causes us to be the first to experience things. Passion drives us to the edge of the movement of God and leaves us asking for more. But passion in itself is not a purpose. Passion is more than a feeling that excites us and moves us to action; it requires purpose in order to exist. When passion has purpose, it becomes functional in our lives.

John was the first to recognize Jesus as the Messiah and the first to die for the gospel as a martyr. We first know of John through the interesting events surrounding his birth. He was the firstborn child of an older priest named Zechariah and his wife, Elizabeth. An angel visited Zechariah and foretold John's birth and his role in the future blessing of the coming Savior.

> All at once an angel from the Lord appeared to Zechariah at the right side of the altar. Zechariah was confused and afraid when he saw the angel.
>
> But the angel told him: "Don't be afraid, Zechariah! God has heard your prayers. Your wife Elizabeth will have a son, and you must name him John. His birth will make you very happy, and many people will be glad. Your son will be a great servant of the Lord. He must never drink wine or beer, and the power of the Holy Spirit will be with him from the time he is born. John will lead many people in Israel to turn back to the Lord their God. He will go ahead of the Lord with the same power and spirit that Elijah had. And because of John, parents will be more thoughtful of their children. And people who now disobey God will begin to think as they ought to. That is how John will get people ready for the Lord" (Luke 1:11-17).

## Making the Mantle

Once Zechariah heard all that the angel said, he showed disbelief by asking how this was possible, since he was old and his wife was beyond childbearing age.

The angel answered, "I am Gabriel, God's servant, and I

was sent to tell you this good news. You have not believed what I have said. So you will not be able to say a thing until all this happens. But everything will take place when it is supposed to" (vv. 19-20).

After years of longing for a child, how could Zechariah have shown disbelief at this angelic announcement? I know, easy for me to say, from my vantage point. But if the presence of an angel wouldn't give you faith, what would? Zechariah's question was very similar to that of both Abraham's and Mary's, but the quality of his disbelief brought about a different result—the loss of his voice.

I believe that God didn't want Zechariah's fear and doubt to affect anyone else, so He closed Zechariah's mouth until the will of God was accomplished. As the saying goes, "If you can't say something good, don't say anything at all."

Eight days after Elizabeth gave birth, she and Zechariah took their child to the Tabernacle to be circumcised, as the law of Moses commanded. When it was time to name the child, everyone assumed he would be called Zechariah, after his father. But Elizabeth told them his name was John. Everyone argued with one another about the lack of history within their family regarding that name. Then they requested a direct response from Zechariah, who asked for a writing tablet and wrote, "His name is John." Immediately his tongue was loosed and he could speak. The first thing Zechariah did was to use his voice to worship the Lord (see Luke 1:57-79).

This was quite a strange and memorable entrance into the world; but John's birth was just the beginning of what in his life would be called strange. John the Baptist became the eccentric prophet in the desert, who ate unusual things and wore camel's hair clothing. He was one man whose heritage would not determine his destiny. John's passion drove him to abandon a highly esteemed role in the priesthood to pursue instead his calling to create a path for the Messiah. His story is a clear example that our passion can drive us—and draw others—to the desert.

> Years later, John the Baptist started preaching in the desert of Judea. He said, "Turn back to God! The kingdom of heaven will soon be here." John was the one the prophet Isaiah was talking about, when he said, "In the desert someone is shouting, 'Get the road ready for the Lord! Make a straight path for him'" (Matt. 3:1-3).

John's shocking approach to ministry and his confrontational message were effective. People were drawn to the desert from all over to hear the message of passionate repentance.

John, though, was more concerned with people's true conversion than he was with drawing big crowds. We see this clearly when he insulted the Pharisees and the Sadducees by calling them snakes. They had come to be baptized, but he knew they believed themselves to be redeemed without repentance, simply because of their bloodline. The interesting point in this is that if anyone had the authority to passionately confront this spirit of religion, it was John. He was as qualified by relation to Abraham as any of the religious leaders, and yet he affirmed the need for repentance, thus fulfilling his purpose to prepare the way for Christ.

## Missing the Mantle

When our passion gets us put in prison, we question everything we know to be true. This is illustrated in the discouragement and vulnerability of John the Baptist when Herod put him in prison. John's passion for conversion made him an enemy when he confronted Herod about Herod's stealing his brother's wife.

> In many different ways John preached the good news to the people. But to Herod the ruler, he said, "It was wrong for you to take Herodias, your brother's wife." John also said that Herod had done many other bad things. Finally, Herod put John in jail, and this was the worst thing he had done. John's followers told John everything that was being said about Jesus. So he sent two of them to ask the Lord, "Are you the one we should be looking for? Or must we wait for someone else?" When the messengers came to Jesus, they said, "John the Baptist sent us to ask, 'Are you the one we should be looking for? Or must we wait for someone else?' " At that time Jesus was healing many people who were sick or in pain or were troubled by evil spirits, and he was giving sight to a lot of blind people. Jesus said to the messengers sent by John, "Go and tell John what you have seen and heard" (Luke 3:18-20; 7:18-22).

Why would John ask a question to which he already knew the answer? When he questioned whether Jesus was the Messiah, he was demonstrating how disillusioned a person can become when imprisoned. This shows that no matter how passionate we might have been about something, when we are threatened we may forget what we once firmly believed. It's only human to be moved by emotion; and in John's case, oppression made him doubt his true belief and knowledge. John knew who Jesus was; he had baptized Jesus and heard the confirmation of Jesus as the Son of God.

While everyone else was being baptized, Jesus himself was baptized. Then as he prayed, the sky opened up, and the Holy Spirit came down upon him in the form of a dove. A voice from heaven said, "You are my own dear Son, and I am pleased with you" (3:21-22).

## Modeling the Mantle

The purpose for passion is to prepare the way for the great work that is to come in and through our lives. John was a symbol of this principle in action. His passion led him to confront others without fear of consequences. He made many enemies through his zealous actions. But in spite of his in-your-face approach, God preserved him and worked through him until his mission was fulfilled. John's mission was accomplished through his empowerment to baptize the Son of God. This event was a touchstone in the spirit realm because it signified the empowerment and blessing of the latest and greatest High Priest (Jesus Christ) by the old system (John's priestly heritage).

Although John and Jesus were blood relatives, their lives were intertwined in the spirit as well. When John led Jesus into baptism, one journey of ministry was ending and another just beginning, as the torch of passion was passed on. John's life is a testimony to the fact that nothing can stop us until we have fulfilled our mission to ignite passion in others. John could have been arrested many times for the things he said to powerful leaders, but God protected him so that he could fulfill his God-given purpose.

All of us who dream of purpose should pray for the passion to possess all God has for us in this life and in the next. Although John did not need acclaim to fuel his mission, it certainly seals his sacrifice in our minds when Jesus later described John by saying, "No one ever born on this earth is greater than John" (7:28).

## Questions to Consider

- ✍ When is the last time you felt the fire of passion?
- ✍ Has your passion ever been held hostage to your circumstances?
- ✍ If so, did you experience depression or disillusionment?

## Authority at a Glance

Wearing the mantle of passion means that

- ✍ your heritage or history does not determine your destiny;
- ✍ your ministry approach may be shocking and your message confrontational, while still being highly effective;
- ✍ you will often be the first to experience things.

## Pattern for Prayer

- ✍ Father, I am thankful for the passion of John the Baptist.
- ✍ The cry of my heart is that Your Spirit will ignite in me the fire of passion.

- Help me make my paths straight for Your coming in my life.
- I long to please You alone.
- I desire passion more than comfort.

## Declarations

- I will choose to take on God's view of my husband.
- I will see my husband wearing the mantle of John.
- I will affirm my husband's passion for God and others.
- I will uphold my role by restoring my husband's authority.
- I will encourage my husband by building him up.

## Seal It with a Gift

I couldn't resist recommending a practical gift for this demonstration. Because John is known as the forerunner of Christ, I am suggesting that you buy your husband tennis shoes. Every time you see your husband wear the shoes, you will be reminded that God is moving passionately in his behalf to make way for the Lord in his life. If you would like to be a bit more passionate yourself, then get some shoes, too! Below are some other suggestions:

- Jogging suit
- Health club membership

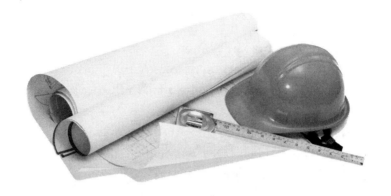

# PETER: THE MANTLE OF STABILITY

*And wisdom and knowledge shall be the stability of thy times, and strength of salvation: the fear of the LORD is his treasure.*
ISAIAH 33:6, *KJV*

To become stable, Peter had to be tested in an unstable environment. It was the only way for him to build internal stability—just as it is for us. Peter's testing was meant to prove his fallibility apart from the knowledge of Christ's identity. In fact, Peter's first name was Simon, meaning "unstable as water." Finding his identity in Christ Jesus was Peter's only source of stability.

# Making the Mantle

Peter had to get out of the boat on two separate occasions. The first time was his introduction to Jesus. When Jesus first found him, Peter was a successful fisherman with influence and friends.

> While Jesus was walking along the shore of Lake Galilee, he saw two brothers. One was Simon, also known as Peter, and the other was Andrew. They were fishermen, and they were casting their net into the lake. Jesus said to them, "Come with me! I will teach you how to bring in people instead of fish." Right then the two brothers dropped their nets and went with him (Matt. 4:18-20).

Peter and Andrew's immediate response is astounding. They must have been intrigued by the offer to catch humans instead of fish. Whatever the reason for their haste, they acted on faith and probably against every thought of responsibility.

Stability was an attribute that fishermen needed if they wanted to provide consistency within their profession. When everything about their job was unpredictable, they could depend on good old-fashioned steadfastness to bring in the catch.

Peter became one of Jesus' most faithful followers and defenders. As far as his career was concerned, he proved that he would take risks when he thought "outside the boat." But he probably never dreamed he would literally step outside the boat and walk on water.

> A little while before morning, Jesus came walking on the water toward his disciples. When they saw him, they thought he was a ghost. They were terrified and started screaming. At once, Jesus said to them, "Don't worry! I

am Jesus. Don't be afraid." Peter replied, "Lord, if it is really you, tell me to come to you on the water." "Come on!" Jesus said. Peter then got out of the boat and started walking on the water toward him. But when Peter saw how strong the wind was, he was afraid and started sinking. "Save me, Lord!" he shouted (14:25-30).

## Missing the Mantle

What made Peter great is also what made him most vulnerable to humiliation. He was quick to believe, but he was also quick to doubt. This was clearly illustrated by his dramatic denial of his relationship with Jesus.

> Jesus said to his disciples, "During this very night, all of you will reject me, as the Scriptures say, 'I will strike down the shepherd, and the sheep will be scattered.' But after I am raised to life, I will go to Galilee ahead of you." Peter spoke up, "Even if all the others reject you, I never will!" Jesus replied, "I promise you that before a rooster crows tonight, you will say three times that you don't know me." But Peter said, "Even if I have to die with you, I will never say I don't know you" (26:31-35).

Peter had faith in himself and his own dependability; but just as the prophets foretold, and as Jesus affirmed, Peter caved in under pressure.

> While Peter was sitting out in the courtyard, a servant girl came up to him and said, "You were with Jesus from Galilee." But in front of everyone Peter said, "That isn't

so! I don't know what you are talking about!" When Peter had gone out to the gate, another servant girl saw him and said to some people there, "This man was with Jesus from Nazareth." Again Peter denied it, and this time he swore, "I don't even know that man!" A little while later some people standing there walked over to Peter and said, "We know that you are one of them. We can tell it because you talk like someone from Galilee." Peter began to curse and swear, "I don't know that man!" Right then a rooster crowed, and Peter remembered that Jesus had said, "Before a rooster crows, you will say three times that you don't know me." Then Peter went out and cried hard (vv. 69-75).

How sad to turn from an adamant declaration of loyalty to the curses of denial, all within a few hours. It doesn't take long to fall. This part of Peter's story shows the fallibility of humankind. No matter how much we desire to be loyal, consistent and full of strength, we fail not because we lack revelation or relationship with God but because we are flawed. Recognition of our flaws takes us back to the place where we can never say "never." We dare not trust in our own integrity, for in God alone will we find strength and stability.

## Modeling the Mantle

Peter is, perhaps, such a likable character to read about because of his similarities to many of us today in the areas of failure and faults. We see Peter high and we see Peter low. When his trust was in himself, he doubted, just as we would. But when he reflected the light of a perfect Savior, his revelation lit up the room.

When Jesus and his disciples were near the town of Caesarea Philippi, he asked them, "What do people say about the Son of Man?" The disciples answered, "Some people say you are John the Baptist or maybe Elijah or Jeremiah or some other prophet." Then Jesus asked them, "But who do you say I am?" Simon Peter spoke up, "You are the Messiah, the Son of the living God."

Jesus told him: "Simon, son of Jonah, you are blessed! You didn't discover this on you own. It was shown to you by my Father in heaven. So I will call you Peter, which means 'a rock.' On this rock I will build my church, and death itself will not have any power over it. I will give you the keys to the kingdom of heaven, and God in heaven will allow whatever you allow on earth. But he will not allow anything that you don't allow" (16:13-19).

Peter's answer placed him as a hero in the faith hall of fame. I can't imagine how good he must have felt to get an answer so perfectly right. But the important nugget of truth in Peter's response to Jesus was how he came to possess this powerful revelation. Jesus said, "You didn't discover this on your own. It was shown to you by my Father in heaven."

Jesus' comment tells us about the hit-or-miss quality of our human nature. We aren't so spiritually adept as we may think. We don't, in our own strength, come to understand the deep mysteries of God. We can learn from Peter's life that we are only as qualified as our level of revelation of Jesus. The kingdom of God was not built on an unstable fisherman but on a fisherman's strong understanding of who Jesus is. With that same understanding, we hold the keys to the Kingdom, and they will bring us connection between heaven and Earth and all the powers therein to bind and loose.

# Questions to Consider

🌿 Has God required that you leave a familiar environment that has brought you stability?

🌿 Can you name a time when you have stepped out of the boat and left your comfort zone?

🌿 How did doubt affect your success?

🌿 Do you really know yourself well enough to trust your responses?

🌿 When you cannot control your environment, do you rely on denial as a way of escape?

🌿 What truth can you profess to keep you stable through times of distress?

# Authority at a Glance

Wearing the mantle of stability means that

🌿 your influence will encourage the success of others;

🌿 you will be a faithful follower and defender of the Kingdom;

🌿 your level of qualification will increase in direct proportion to your understanding of who Jesus is.

# Pattern for Prayer

🌿 Father, I give You the right to establish Your kingdom in my heart.

🌿 Keep my focus on You, Lord.

- Protect my mind with a complete revelation of who You are.
- My commitment is to grow in You.

## Declarations

- I will choose to take on God's view of my husband.
- I will see my husband wearing the mantle of Peter.
- I will affirm my husband as the stability in our family.
- I will uphold my role by restoring my husband's authority.
- I will encourage my husband by building him up.

## Seal It with a Gift

Stability is as constant as time itself. Because of this, I recommend a timepiece for the demonstration of this mantle.

- A wristwatch
- A desk clock
- An hourglass

# CHAPTER 19

# PAUL: THE MANTLE OF PURPOSE

*And we know that all things work together for good to them that love*
*God, to them who are the called according to his purpose.*
ROMANS 8:28, *KJV*

Saul's conversion to Paul the apostle was the most dramatic conversion in Scripture. He went from pursuing Christians and executing them to teaching and mentoring them in the ways of God and His purpose for a personal relationship with them. Before his conversion, Saul was an effective adversary against the kingdom of God, even presiding over the death of Stephen, who was stoned as a martyr.

The council members shouted and covered their ears. At once they all attacked Stephen and dragged him out of the city. Then they started throwing stones at him. The men who had brought charges against him put their coats at the feet of a young man named Saul. Saul approved the stoning of Stephen (Acts 7:57-58; 8:1).

# Making the Mantle

Saul was a dangerous man who held stringently to his purpose of participating in the annihilation of believers in Christ. He spent many years working as a public official because he was trained in the Law of the Scriptures.

> At that time the church in Jerusalem suffered terribly. All of the Lord's followers, except the apostles, were scattered everywhere in Judea and Samaria. Saul started making a lot of trouble for the church. He went from house to house, arresting men and women and putting them in jail (8:1-3).

And then, on the road to Damascus, the light of revelation brought Saul to his knees.

> Saul kept on threatening to kill the Lord's followers. He even went to the high priest and asked for letters to their leaders in Damascus. He did this because he wanted to arrest and take to Jerusalem any man or woman who had accepted the Lord's Way. When Saul had almost reached Damascus, a bright light from heaven suddenly flashed around him. He fell to the ground and heard a voice that said, "Saul! Saul! Why are you so cruel to me?" "Who are you?" Saul asked. "I am Jesus," the Lord answered. "I am

the one you are so cruel to. Now get up and go into the city, where you will be told what to do." The men with Saul stood there speechless. They had heard the voice, but they had not seen anyone. Saul got up from the ground, and when he opened his eyes, he could not see a thing. Someone then led him by the hand to Damascus, and for three days he was blind and did not eat or drink (9:1-9).

After Saul's initial change of direction, God called a man named Ananias to take Saul through the transformation process. After Ananias first reminded God of the danger of this man, Ananias then listened to the Lord's instruction.

The Lord said to Ananias, "Go! I have chosen him to tell foreigners, kings, and the people of Israel about me. I will show him how much he must suffer for worshiping in my name." Ananias left and went into the house where Saul was staying. Ananias placed his hands on him and said, "Saul, the Lord Jesus has sent me. He is the same one who appeared to you along the road. He wants you to be able to see and to be filled with the Holy Spirit." Suddenly something like fish scales fell from Saul's eyes, and he could see. He got up and was baptized (vv. 15-18).

## Missing the Mantle

The ultimate vulnerability of all men and women is misguided purpose. The beginning of Paul's life shows us how focused a person can become on a purpose that is not Holy Spirit led, and the subsequent destruction that follows. Before Jesus' revelation to him, Saul had a full knowledge of the Scriptures and the law of Moses; but his knowledge did not have the power to save him. What he was missing was the purpose for which every word of Scripture had been written—revelation of Jesus Christ, the Son of the living God. Saul thought himself religious and zealous for the God of Abraham, but he had been deceived into defending only a shell of revelation. He later found that his actions were contrary to the plan of God.

When pursuing the purpose of God, personal pride is our greatest enemy. It is what causes us to be fueled by a sense of accomplishment that can hinder our high calling and ultimately cause us to miss the mark. The definition of "sin" is "missing the mark of the purpose for which we were created." Scripture says, "All of us have sinned and fallen short of God's glory" (Rom. 3:23). Until we have a face-to-face meeting with the Son of God, we may be aimlessly working to destroy, instead of pursue, our purpose in Christ. Perhaps this eternal principle is best shown in the complete humility we see in the life of a purposeful Paul—the man who spent the remainder of his life restoring and building up the kingdom he had earlier fought to destroy.

## Modeling the Mantle

I have been to the prison in Rome where Paul was held in chains. I call it the humility hole, because it is little more than a hole in the ground. During the time he was kept there, the only way to enter was to be lowered through a narrow circle in the ground. Now there is a modest staircase to give some assistance. I wept as I stood hunched over in the short space of that cell and imagined what it must have been like for the great apostle. I also realized that God puts us in places that we would not choose in order to accomplish an eternal goal. Paul suffered imprisonment on several occasions; and had he not been arrested, he would likely have continued to travel from church to church, keeping busy with the day-to-day work of being an Early Church apostle. But God had a much greater legacy for Paul to leave. By keeping him imprisoned, God led Paul to use the only form of communication he could—the written word.

Paul never lost sight of his purpose, in spite of his surroundings. He could have become angry because God didn't shake the prison down as He had done for Peter. But there was godly purpose for the differing outcomes of these two men of God. We can glory in the resulting eternal reward of humility, which is the ultimate purpose of God. If Paul had not been in prison, he would have occupied himself with other acts of purpose; but only God knew that the letters he wrote from prison would lead us to find our purpose today.

## Questions to Consider

- ✍ Have you ever sincerely thought that you were right about something and it turned out you were wrong?
- ✍ Have you ever been stopped or severely corrected by God?
- ✍ Would you desire to see God face-to-face, even if it meant you would lose something valuable?
- ✍ Has a season of separation closed you off to business as usual but made you all the more creative?

## Authority at a Glance

Wearing the mantle of purpose means that

- ✍ your life will dramatically change as you follow God's will;
- ✍ you may do many things well and still miss the mark of the purpose for which you were created;
- ✍ you will understand that knowledge is nothing without the support of passion and purpose.

## Pattern for Prayer

- ✍ Father, thank You for taking my life to a new level.
- ✍ I submit all my plans to You.
- ✍ Guide my every step.
- ✍ My hope is in Your purpose for me.
- ✍ I believe that all things work together for good to those of us who are called according to His purpose (see Rom. 8:28).

## Declarations

- ✍ I will choose to take on God's view of my husband.
- ✍ I will see my husband wearing the mantle of Paul.
- ✍ I will affirm my husband's calling and his purpose.
- ✍ I will uphold my role by restoring my husband's authority.
- ✍ I will encourage my husband by building him up.

## Seal It with a Gift

The best practice for believers to discover their purpose is charting their course. This can be done in several ways; here are my recommendations:

- A journal for writing your mission statement and tracking your thoughts and experiences
- A globe or decorative map to remind you to receive God's purpose
- A road trip to a destination that can teach or help identify purpose through observation (for example, a state capitol or the place of your family origin)

# Function by Design

**Design goal:** To formulate a functional furniture floor plan

I have a living room in the center of my house that has posed a real dilemma in designing a functional floor plan. This room has five different points of entry, floor-to-ceiling windows, a see-through serving bar and a fireplace. I wanted this room to be comfortable and accommodating without blocking the doors, windows and fireplace. I achieved all of my goals by "floating" (placing away from the walls) my primary seating—a loveseat and sofa—one coffee table and end table. The loveseat runs parallel to the shortest wall in the room, while the main sofa runs parallel to the longer wall. I created a secondary seating circle with two chairs; both chairs face inward so that conversation from the couch grouping would also include them. Yet one chair faces the armoire and serves as a television viewing chair; the other serves as a reading chair with a lamp beside it.

A functional furniture floor plan truly transforms a room. Function can be fluidly achieved by laying out a room with two goals in mind: preserving conversation space and achieving convenient traffic flow. The following steps are the same ones I used to find the perfect seating arrangement for my challenging room:

1.  Brainstorm on paper by laying out your floor plan; then clear the room of small items, including all pictures. Removing everything is very important, since this will change your perspective. You will rehang pictures after you have all the furniture in place.

Note: Do not crowd furniture around doorways or in the flow of traffic; it is best to move those pieces of furniture to another room.

2. To create your first circle of furniture, move your three to five largest pieces of furniture to the proposed location before moving any other seating or small items. Your goal is to provide sanctuary seating for a furniture group; that is, seating that encourages conversation but does not hinder traffic patterns. Note: If every wall in a living area is broken up with windows, doors, walkways, fireplaces or televisions, then float your furniture by bringing it to the center of the room.

3. Armoires and bookcases can form a second circle of furniture in a room. This circle adds dimension. Consider adding a couple of chairs or a single reading chair and lamp to this second circle, which will expand your seating when you entertain.

4. If the bulk of your furniture functions better on one side of the room, balance can be achieved by adding a large piece of artwork or cluster of pictures above a narrow buffet or sofa table (to conserve walking space) on the opposite side of the room. Color and texture will bring balance.

PART 7

*Design Element:*

# ILLUMINATION

*Light does more than banish darkness. It can bathe a room in a soft glow, sparkle across a table set with crystal and silver and bounce off of polished wood floors, picking up color and texture all the way. Light displays energy and motion even when it seems to be perfectly still.*
MARTHA STEWART

The need for lighting can be divided into two different types: mood lighting and task lighting. Minimal light is used to set a mood, while task lighting requires more light to help in the completion of jobs around the house. This is why we want subtle lamps and candles in our living rooms and bedrooms. These forms of light make us feel warm, cozy and relaxed, thereby putting us in a favorable mood. When we need to cook, clean or do school work, our need to perform a function demands greater visibility.

The Word of God is illumination to our spirits. In the same way that our need for light determines the type of lighting we use, our need for revelation determines how and where we apply God's Word. When we are in need of a mood lift, we use a little of the Word and we are renewed; but the amount of revelation to lift our spirits is not enough to light our path to progress. When we are called on to fulfill a commission given to us by God, we need all the light we can get. So let us walk in the light of the Word of God and be filled with illumination.

# CHAPTER 20

# JESUS: THE MANTLE OF ILLUMINATION

*As long as I am in the world, I am the light of the world.*
JOHN 9:5, *NKJV*

*I am the light of the world: he that followeth me shall not walk in darkness, but shall have the light of life.*
JOHN 8:12, *KJV*

*Never again will there be any night. No one will need lamplight or sunlight. The shining of God, the Master, is all the light anyone needs. And they will rule with him age after age after age.*
REVELATION 22:5, *THE MESSAGE*

# Jesus Illuminates Perspective

Jesus Christ is everything we need in a man, all wrapped up in one bright package. When He entered our world, every experience and every purpose became illuminated through Him. And it is only through Jesus, as the focal point of our lives, that we establish and maintain proper perspective.

> Don't shuffle along, eyes to the ground, absorbed with the things right in front of you. Look up, and be alert to what is going on around Christ—that's where the action is. See things from his perspective (Col. 3:2, *THE MESSAGE*).

# Jesus Illuminates Unity

The longest prayer of Jesus recorded in Scripture is found in John 17; its focus expresses our Lord's desire for unity among His followers.

> I in them and you in me. May they be brought to complete unity to let the world know that you sent me and have loved them even as you have loved me (v. 23, *NIV*).

Not only did Jesus pray for unity, but He also modeled unity through His faithfulness, His obedience and His determination.

- **Jesus was faithful:** "Jesus was faithful to God, who appointed him, just as Moses was faithful in serving all of God's people. But Jesus deserves more honor than Moses, just as the builder of a house deserves more honor than the house. Of course, every house is built by someone, and God is really the one who built everything" (Heb. 3:2-4).

- **Jesus was obedient:** "And being found in fashion as a man, he humbled himself, and became obedient unto death, even the death of the cross" (Phil. 2:8, *KJV*).

- **Jesus was determined:** "Looking unto Jesus the author and finisher of our faith; who for the joy that was set before him endured the cross, despising the shame, and is set down at the right hand of the throne of God" (Heb. 12:2, *KJV*).

## Jesus Illuminates Creativity

Through the mighty works of His hands—miracles—Jesus illuminated God's creativity.

Jesus went all over Galilee, teaching in the Jewish meeting places and preaching the good news about God's kingdom. He also healed every kind of disease and sickness. News about him spread all over Syria, and people with every kind of sickness or disease were brought to him. . . . Jesus healed them all (Matt. 4:23-24).

Jesus performed miracles as He looked to the future, communicated God's truth and walked in submission to the Father.

- **Jesus dreamed of the future:** "Right after those days of suffering, 'The sun will become dark, and the moon will no longer shine. The stars will fall, and the powers in the sky will be shaken.' Then a sign will appear in the sky. And there will be the Son of Man. All nations on earth will weep when they see the Son of Man coming on the clouds of heaven with power and great glory. At the sound of a loud trumpet, he will send his angels to bring his chosen ones together from all over the earth" (24:29-31).

⍅ **Jesus was a great communicator:** "When Jesus was alone with the twelve apostles and some others, they asked him about these stories. He answered: "I have explained the secret about God's kingdom to you, but for others I can use only stories" (Mark 4:10-11).

⍅ **Jesus walked in submission:** "I tell you for certain that the Son cannot do anything on his own. He can do only what he sees the Father doing, and he does exactly what he sees the Father do. I cannot do anything on my own. The Father sent me, and he is the one who told me how to judge. I judge with fairness, because I obey him, and I don't just try to please myself" (John 5:19,30).

## Jesus Illuminates Authenticity

No one better represented authenticity than Jesus, who illuminated the authentic likeness of God in everything He said and did. Jesus was real in His experiences and transparent about His temptations.

We have a great high priest, who has gone into heaven, and he is Jesus the Son of God. That is why we must hold on to what we have said about him. Jesus understands every weakness of ours, because he was tempted in every way that we are. But he did not sin! So whenever we are in need, we should come bravely before the throne of our merciful God. There we will be treated with underserved kindness, and we will find help (Heb. 4:14-16).

- ✍ **Jesus was dedicated:** "Jesus is God's own Son, but still he had to suffer before he could learn what it really means to obey God. Suffering made Jesus perfect, and now he can save forever all who obey him" (5:8-9).
- ✍ **Jesus worshiped:** "God had the power to save Jesus from death. And while Jesus was on earth, he begged God with loud crying and tears to save him. He truly worshiped God, and God listened to his prayers" (v. 7).
- ✍ **Jesus was wise:** "Jesus answered, 'Why did you have to look for me? Didn't you know that I would be in my Father's house?' But they did not understand what he meant. Jesus went back to Nazareth with his parents and obeyed them. His mother kept on thinking about all that had happened. Jesus became wise, and he grew strong. God was pleased with him and so were the people" (Luke 2:49-52).

## Jesus Illuminates Balance

Keeping our focus on Jesus, who led a perfectly balanced life, will enable us to be balanced in our own approach to life and ministry.

Dear friends, do not believe every spirit, but test the spirits to see whether they are from God, because many false prophets have gone out into the world. This is how you can recognize the Spirit of God: Every spirit that acknowledges that Jesus Christ has come in the flesh is from God, but every spirit that does not acknowledge Jesus is not from God. This is the spirit of the antichrist, which you have heard is coming and even now is already in the world (1 John 4:1-3, *NIV*).

- **Jesus was confrontational:** "Not long before the Jewish festival of Passover, Jesus went to Jerusalem. There he found people selling cattle, sheep, and doves in the temple. He also saw moneychangers sitting at their tables. So he took some rope and made a whip. Then he chased everyone out of the temple, together with their sheep and cattle. He turned over the tables of the moneychangers and scattered their coins. Jesus said to the people who had been selling doves, 'Get those doves out of here! Don't make my Father's house a marketplace'" (John 2:13-16).

- **Jesus interpreted mysteries:** "As Jesus was leaving the temple, one of his disciples said to him, 'Teacher, look at these beautiful stones and wonderful buildings!' Jesus replied, 'Do you see these huge buildings? They will certainly be torn down! Not one stone will be left in place.' Later, as Jesus was sitting on the Mount of Olives across from the temple, Peter, James, John and Andrew came to him in private. They asked, 'When will these things happen? What will be the sign that they are about to take place?'" (Mark 13:1-

3). Jesus answered them, revealing the mysteries of the coming age in verses 5-30 of the same chapter.

ॐ **Jesus was an effective leader:** "When Jesus saw the large crowd coming toward him, he asked Philip, 'Where will we get enough food to feed all these people?' He said this to test Philip, since he already knew what he was going to do. The ground was covered with grass, and Jesus told his disciples to have everyone sit down. About five thousand men were in the crowd. Jesus took the bread in his hands and gave thanks to God. Then he passed the bread to the people, and he did the same with the fish, until everyone had plenty to eat" (John 6:5-6,10-11).

## Jesus Illuminates Function

Anytime we find ourselves questioning our purpose or function in the Body of Christ, we need only look at Jesus to see how clearly God has called and gifted each of us for His perfect purpose.

Just as each of us has one body with many members, and these members do not all have the same function, so in Christ we who are many form one body, and each member belongs to all the others. We have different gifts, according to the grace given us (Rom. 12:4-6, *NIV*).

ॐ **Jesus had passion:** "Father, I want everyone you have given me to be with me, wherever I am. Then they will see the glory that you have given me, because you loved me before the world was created. Good Father, the people of this world don't know you. But I know you, and my followers know that you sent me. I told them what you are like, and I will tell them even more. Then the love that you have for me will become part of them, and I will be one with them" (John 17:24-26).

- ∞ **Jesus had stability:** "We must keep our eyes on Jesus, who leads us and makes our faith complete. He endured the shame of being nailed to a cross, because he knew that later on he would be glad he did. Now he is seated at the right side of God's throne! So keep your mind on Jesus, who put up with many insults from sinners. Then you won't get discouraged and give up" (Heb. 12:2-3).

- ∞ **Jesus had purpose:** "Jesus knew that the Father had put all things under his power, and that he had come from God and was returning to God" (John 13:3, *NIV*).

## Pattern for Prayer

- ∞ Jesus, You are the lamp unto my feet and the light unto my path (see Ps. 119:105).
- ∞ Thank You for Your Word, which illuminates.
- ∞ Your Word helps me see the flaws in my nature, as well as the greatness You have placed in me.
- ∞ I am grateful for the ability to see You, Jesus, at work in my life.

## Seal It with a Gift

Jesus brings light to every home where He is welcomed. To demonstrate your hospitality to the Holy Spirit, focus your attention on different forms of light. My favorite gift to give or receive is a candle.

- Scented candle or a candelabra
- Book light
- Decorative lamp

# Illumination by Design

**Design goal:** Create a focused lamplight with custom lampshades

Many people tend to buy white or off-white lamp shades, which diffuse light in every direction. Most of these plain lampshades can be covered with fabric and trim to customize them to a room's decor. As an added benefit, they darken the color of the shade light, focusing it downward to bring attention to special areas. Beautiful custom lamps are one of the simplest yet most extravagantly beautiful additions to any room. And once you have this creative edge, you will be able to save lots of money, while adding mood lighting in whichever room you choose.

Round pleated shades cannot be used for this exercise. Paneled shades are the best. The items needed are these:

- 1 lampshade
- 1 8x10-inch piece of paper
- Scissors
- 1 yard of fabric or a ½ yard of two different prints of fabric
- Spray fabric adhesive
- Flat braided edging
- Hot-glue gun
- Loop fringe for trim on top and bottom

1. Prepare your lampshade by removing prefab raised trim or cording that separates the panels from the trim (these will be replaced with flat braid).
2. Lay the piece of paper over one panel of the shade and press the edges around corners to leave a print on the paper.

3. Cut the panel impression out of the paper.

4. Place paper pattern on fabric and cut out fabric for each panel side (test one panel against the lamp before cutting them all).

5. If using two patterns, lay them in an alternating pattern in a row.

6. Spray the back of one piece of fabric with spray adhesive and apply by pressing the top down first, then work your way downward.

7. Don't be afraid of overlap or shortage as long as it is minimal; it will be covered by trim.

8. Continue to glue each fabric piece onto the panels.

9. Cut the braid trim for vertical edging between panels.

10. Hot-glue each vertical braid trim to the shade.

11. Measure and cut loop fringe for the top and bottom of the shade by guiding it along the edge.

12. Hot-glue the loop fringe to the top and again to the bottom of the shade to finish it off.

This technique is great for recovering small shades for your dining room or kitchen chandelier using your chair or curtain fabric. In fact, I advise that you practice using scrap fabric and trim on a small shade to be sure you have the steps down just right before you cut into expensive fabric. Just remember to adjust the scale of your fabric print and trim size smaller or larger, based on the size of the shade. You don't want your trim to overwhelm your small shade, or look small and dinky on a large shade.

Lamps create ambience in many places, such as the kitchen and bathroom countertops, entryway tables, window seats.

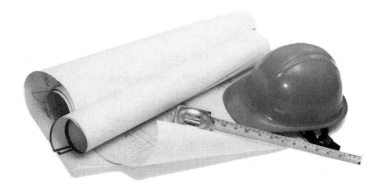

# ARE YOU READY FOR THE BIG "REVEAL"?

*For now we see through a glass, darkly; but then face to face: now I know in part; but then shall I know even as also I am known.*
1 CORINTHIANS 13:12, *KJV*

I love the design frenzy we are experiencing right now on television. I think it is wonderful for the mainstream public to see the importance of making their homes beautiful, functional and unique. In my opinion, the most exciting part of these shows is the "reveal" at the end. Hours upon hours of vision and labor all come down to one moment when the homeowners' get to see the end result of their home's makeover.

You are about to experience many eye-opening moments in your marriage! God is waiting with anticipation for the time when you will see all the changes that have taken place under the cover of your prayer. You can be confident of your investment. In fact, praying for your husband and making declarations of restoration is a lifelong investment that continues to pave the way into the future.

Your husband is lucky to have you as his wife and spiritual companion! The reverse side of your investment is that you are a lucky woman to be married to a man who has been the subject of so much prayer and attention. Not only have you turned *your* attention and focus on him, but due to the influx of prayer on his behalf, *all of heaven* has fallen in line to watch over the Word of God in his life and perform it. This is also true for single women. Your prayers now will definitely make a difference in the man you marry; but they may also affect the time frame in which you meet him, since you will be helping him prepare for marriage, too!

## Put Your Knowledge into Action

To maintain what you have built through proper perspective and focused prayer, I admonish you to continually put your knowledge into action. In the past year, God has answered so many of my prayers by isolating the real issues and uprooting them. Some major upheavals have been avoided because of the preparation of prayer laid out before my husband and me. Be encouraged by the instruction of Jesus:

> I will show you what he is like who comes to me and hears my words and puts them into practice. He is like a

man building a house, who dug down deep and laid the foundation on rock. When a flood came, the torrent struck that house but could not shake it, because it was well built (Luke 6:47-48, *NIV*).

If you begin to feel discouraged, you can turn it around quickly by declaring your gratitude for all God has done and will do in your life. The Lucky Lady Declaration can help. It is simple and effective in reminding us of the knowledge and actions that bring us well-being.

### Lucky Lady Declaration (Married Women)

- I am a lucky lady!
- I am blessed because I honor my husband as the spiritual leader of our home.
- I am at peace walking in obedience to the will of God.
- I am protected in the position of submission.
- I am passionate about praying for my husband.
- I am grateful to be his wife.
- I am a lucky lady to have my life!

### Lucky Lady Declaration (Single Women)

- I am a lucky lady!
- I am blessed because I faithfully trust the timing of God.
- I am at peace walking in obedience to the will of God.
- I am protected as a princess of the Most High.
- I am passionate about preparing for my husband to be.

- I will be ready to be his wife!
- I am a lucky lady to have my life!

How could we ask for more than blessing, peace, protection, passion and gratefulness? Not only does this declaration remind us of what we may be missing when we fall out of step, but it also lets us know how to reclaim what should be ours!

## Go with the Flow

Now that you have read through the book and prayed the mantles in the order of reading about them, I want you to ask the Holy Spirit to show you which mantles to return to for spending a little more time praying over your husband. In fact, you could take this book a step further by studying other men or women of God and following the same system of prayer and declaration.

## Don't Stop Declaring

Now that you have fully taken possession of the tool of declaration, keep on using it to forge the future. You can turn almost any Scripture into a powerful declaration. (I recommend using Psalms and Proverbs as guides.) By memorizing special declarations, you arm yourself for the tricks and the traps of the Enemy. You also hone your "honor skills" by following a script when dealing with sticky spousal situations. You know what those situations are. They don't have to be a big deal to be an opportunity to blow it in a big way.

Thank you for your investment of time in reading this book

and reflecting on the questions and exercises. I hope this has been an encouragement to you and maybe a bit fun as well. We can never go wrong when we use the Word of God to build up our most treasured possessions—the ones we love.

I want to end this book by praying over you.

- *⚘* Father God, I thank You for the great woman you have designed.
- *⚘* From head to toe she has been made in Your likeness.
- *⚘* God, I ask You to lead her to a greater level of empowerment.
- *⚘* Show Yourself strong on her behalf. Make her increasingly aware of Your perspective and will in her life and in the lives of those around her.
- *⚘* I ask You to pour upon her a double portion of wisdom and wealth, in the spirit realm and in the natural realm, as a sign of Your faithfulness to those who diligently seek You.
- *⚘* Lord, allow Your grace to envelop her as she walks in truth and discipline and desires to do Your perfect will. Amen!

# Leave a Legacy That Will Last a Lifetime

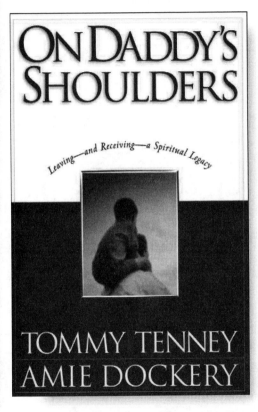

**On Daddy's Shoulders**
Leaving—and Receiving—a Spiritual Legacy
*Tommy Tenney* and *Amie Dockery*
ISBN 08307.27930

Both Amie Dockery and Tommy Tenney, the best-selling author of The God Chasers series, are the recipients of generational blessings. In *On Daddy's Shoulders,* the two have come together to inspire a legacy of passionate pursuit of God. Every godly parent desires their offspring to reach higher and see further than they have seen. This wonderful book highlights the importance of leaving a heritage and receiving blessing generation to generation.

As the authors explain, when we are children, we learn to dance by standing on Daddy's shoes. But as we grow and mature, we stand on his shoulders, balancing our lives on the foundation of parental teaching. Our heavenly Father has also promised us a legacy— a blessing that flows from generation to generation.

Who will provide this legacy to your children? With the inspiring guidance found in *On Daddy's Shoulders,* you will.

# Inspiring Reading
## for Women

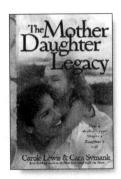

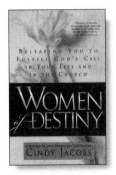